THE BEST OF

Birds & Blooms

Ruby-throated hummingbird, page 34

Table of Contents

ON THE FRONT COVER
Eastern bluebird. Photo by Steve and Dave Maslowski

ON THE TITLE PAGE
Cedar waxwing. Photo by William Leaman/Alamy Stock Photo

Contributors

Lisa Ballard, Sheryl DeVore, Emily Hannemann, Mark E. Hauber, Kenn and Kimberly Kaufman, Ken Keffer, Heather Lamb, Rachel Maidl, Luke Miller, Melinda Myers, Kelsey Roseth, Sally Roth, Jill Staake, Kaitlin Stainbrook, Deb Wiley

1610 N. 2nd St., Suite 102, Milwaukee, WI 53212-3906

International Standard Book Number:
D 978-1-62145-702-2
U 978-1-62145-703-9

Component Number:
D 118500102H
U 118500104H

International Standard Serial Number: 1553-8400

Printed in USA
1 3 5 7 9 10 8 6 4 2

Fiery skipper butterfly, page 195

Welcome!

We'd like to introduce you to the new edition of *The Best of Birds & Blooms,* which will get you out bird-watching, learning about and attracting new species, growing healthy plants and more.

Have you ever wondered why birds sing after a storm? Find out on page 235. Or read about a touching way to memorialize people and milestones in your life with trees and plants on page 170. Plus, there are so many photos of hummingbirds and butterflies!

Get inspired here and get outside to do what makes you happy.

—THE EDITORS OF *BIRDS & BLOOMS* MAGAZINE

Red crossbills, page 93

CHAPTER 1

Backyard Bird-Watching

Find out how to attract the most sought-after species to your own landscape.

Best Singers

From melodic calls to zipping chips, birds delight with their sounds. Listen for these top songsters as you are birding in your own backyard.

Eastern meadowlark

◀ MEADOWLARKS

Despite the "lark" part of their name, meadowlarks are related to blackbirds. Males are known to sit on prominent perches and belt out bright whistling tunes. The western meadowlark, official bird of six states, proclaims a pure melody followed by a short jumbled phrase. Eastern meadowlarks sing a similar fluted tune but lack the closing bubbly notes. Where their ranges overlap along the Great Plains, the difference in song helps minimize hybridization. It also serves as the easiest way to identify these two look-alikes.

▶ RED-WINGED BLACKBIRDS

For some, the raspy *conk-ah-reeeee* of red-winged blackbirds is a sign of spring. Males return from wintering ranges to claim breeding territories in wetland marshes before the females return. The males actively defend territories, not just against other birds but from anything that dares to get too close, including people. As much as a quarter of a blackbird's day is spent monitoring area boundaries and accosting intruders. Calling red-wings also flash their red-and-yellow wing epaulets in a visual display to attract mates and warn rivals.

▲ WOOD THRUSHES

Wood thrushes make one of the classic sounds of eastern deciduous forests: spirally flute notes that reverberate off the trees. Thrushes and some other birds can even sing two notes simultaneously, thanks to a two-branched vocal organ called a syrinx. The beautiful and melodic self-harmonizing is especially evident on the third phrase of the *ee-oh-lay* of the wood thrush song. As wooded areas become fragmented, the small timber-dwelling birds are experiencing population declines across their range.

▶ NORTHERN CARDINALS

Cardinals have a beautiful song to match their vibrant colors. A metallic *chip* reveals their presence in dense thickets throughout the year, but spring brings out the lovely, repetitive song of the species. The males and females sing lilting duets. Their call-and-response tunes are thought to reinforce pair bonds. Sometimes females even sing from the nest. Lure cardinals to backyards with sunflower or safflower seeds. Platform feeders are especially attractive to these hefty-bodied and cheerful songsters.

◀ AMERICAN ROBINS

The most common of the three thrushes on this list, American robins whistle out the familiar *cheery up, cheery oh* tune. The repeated notes rise and then fall. Early birds get the worm, and few species are up as early as robins. They kick off a sunrise serenade well before the first rays of light. Plant native berries to attract robins to your area. While they rarely use feeders, they do snack on mealworms or fruits. A simple nesting platform also encourages these popular spring singers to make your yard their stage.

▼ NORTHERN MOCKINGBIRDS

They're widespread in the southern and eastern United States, but northern mockingbirds show up nearly anywhere in the country. Their vast vocal range is the result of lifelong learning, with the birds eventually imitating dozens of sounds. Mockingbirds don't limit their singing to sunrise. They continue to call throughout the day and sometimes well into the night. Unmated males sing most frequently. Females also sing, although theirs is a softer tune. Mockingbird repertoires boast different sets for spring and fall—spring singing is for breeding, while fall tunes help establish prime wintering territories.

▲ CHICKADEES

Days are always brightened by the cheery sounds of chickadees. Most utter the usual *chick-a-dee-dee-dee* proclamation. The black-capped chickadee (above) sings out a pure whistling *cheese-bur-ger*. In the Southeast, Carolina chickadees sing a rolling four-note *drink your root beer*. Because chickadees often travel in mixed flocks with other species, listening for their chatter can help you find nuthatches, warblers and downy woodpeckers, too. Watch for chickadees darting in to grab one seed at a time from your feeders.

► VEERIES

Veeries are very similar to wood thrushes. Both species belt out amazing songs and share rich cinnamon red coloration, although the veery's spots on its underparts are less distinct and limited to its chest. The song of the veery is a breezy downward-spiraling whistle. The birds breed in northern forest habitats with dense understories, so migration is the best time to see one. They may occasionally show up in woodlots or backyards during spring and fall movements.

MEADOWLARK, MOCKINGBIRD: STEVE AND DAVE MASLOWSKI; BLACKBIRD, CARDINAL, VEERY: WILLIAM LEAMAN/THE IMAGE FINDERS;

▲ CAROLINA WRENS

Wrens are vocally boisterous, and the portly Carolina wrens are no exception. Their song is often described as *teakettle*, but male wrens cycle through a repertoire of various phrasing. Pairs of Carolina wrens stay together, nesting in cavities and defending their territory throughout the year. In winter, they're occasionally found as far north as southern Canada. Support populations in the northern end of the range by putting out suet feeders during short cold snaps.

IN THE THICKETS

Gray catbirds are at home in low vines and thick brush. They're difficult to spot, but keep an eye out for males in spring. They often perch on top of shrubs and call out to defend their territory.

The Cat's Meow

Put out fresh fruit, plant berry-filled shrubs and listen for gray catbirds in early spring.

IF YOU HEAR something that sounds like a cat screeching in the distance interspersed with bubbly chirping, you might wonder what all of the commotion is about. It's probably a gray catbird doing what it does best: singing.

The catbird's call is—to say the least—distinctive. But that harsh sound imitating a cat's meow is just one of the noises these singers make. Catbirds carry more than 100 different tunes, ranging from crooning to mimicry. That ability runs in the family. As a member of the Mimidae family, the catbird is closely related to mockingbirds and brown thrashers.

"You can tell a catbird's song because it's very long and highly variable," explains Mike Webster, director of the Cornell Lab of Ornithology's Macaulay Library. "It sounds improvised, and they tend not to repeat notes, whereas a mockingbird will repeat notes several times."

Once you find where the noise is coming from, look for a slate gray, medium-sized bird with a black cap and a patch of reddish brown under the tail. Males and females appear identical, but males sing much more frequently. Energetic and lively, catbirds actively hop from branch to shrub to tree, never staying still for long.

Catbirds spend their winters along the eastern and southern coasts of the United States, as well as in tropical areas like Guatemala and Mexico. Come spring and summer, they settle throughout the U.S., with the exception of parts of the West and Southwest. They prefer vines, shrubs and other plants that offer plenty of cover.

It's unusual to see a group of catbirds flocking together. Instead, a mating couple might call your backyard home, returning to the same nesting site every year.

Once she's paired, the female constructs a nest with materials her mate brings, like twigs, paper, weeds, grass and leaves. A careful builder, she skillfully layers those findings so the finest are on the inside while the heavy-duty stuff protects the outside. She lays three or four eggs and incubates them for about two weeks. Babies fledge after a week or two, but the parents help them find food for up to 12 days after they leave the nest.

To attract catbirds to your backyard, plant shrubs or young trees. They don't normally munch on birdseed; their favorite snack is berries. They especially enjoy the fruit from dogwood, winterberry and serviceberry plants.

If you don't have room or happen to be looking for a less-permanent option, put up oriole feeders full of fresh oranges or offer fruit-based jellies or jams. Catbirds are also drawn to raisins, peanut butter and fruit-flavored suet.

BUZZ OFF!

Although many birds allow outsiders on their turf in winter, gray catbirds are extremely territorial and protect their space even when the cold has set in. To scare off trespassers, they fluff themselves up, spread their tails and open their bills.

"In his whole life he has never missed the rising of the sun. He dislikes snow. But a few raisins give him the greatest delight."

Mary Oliver
CATBIRD

COMMUNICATION IS KEY

Males are more vocal, but during breeding season, a female may complete a male's song to form a duet. This behavior serves several purposes, including letting their mate know they're close to the nest.

FROM LEFT: MARIE READ; ELLIOTTE RUSTY HAROLD/SHUTTERSTOCK

A female orchard oriole at a sugar-water feeder.

NECTAR ROBBERS

Orioles and hummingbirds love nectar, and they pollinate flowers by inadvertently transferring pollen from bloom to bloom as they feed. Orchard orioles sometimes bypass a flower's pollen entirely, piercing the flower's base and getting a taste for free.

TINY FLIER

The orchard is the smallest of the eight oriole species found north of Mexico. It has a wingspan of a little more than 9 inches, a few inches larger than a yellow warbler. For comparison, the Baltimore oriole's wingspan is nearly 12 inches.

ORCHARD ORIOLE RANGE MAP

Orange in the Orchard

Attract a pair of vibrant nectar-loving orchard orioles with sweet treats.

EAST OF THE ROCKIES, an oriole that's smaller and much darker than a Baltimore dashes through the flowering trees. The bird you've spotted is probably an orchard oriole. The two birds share similar markings, but where a male Baltimore oriole has a bright pop of orange, the orchard oriole sports a darker chestnut color.

Female orchard and Baltimore orioles look alike, too. They share a warm-hued chest, head and tail feathers, but the female Baltimore has touches of tangerine orange while the orchard's color runs closer to greenish yellow.

Female orchard orioles are the primary nest builders (though their mates may sometimes help out), constructing their homes in forks of branches. Over the course of a week, they weave grass and other flexible plant fibers into a pouch or a basket. Then they line the nests with softer plant down, feathers and the occasional piece of yarn.

Unlike other birds, orchard orioles will share their territory in the summer. In fact, one tree may hold several nesting pairs. They build their homes alongside other bird species, too, such as American robins, eastern kingbirds and the look-alike Baltimore orioles.

Orchard orioles usually prefer open woodlands, lakeshores, parks, farms and, of course, orchards. They spend time in treetops and bushes, where they forage for protein-packed insects and spiders with their sharp, thin beaks.

Early May is the perfect time to attract orchard orioles as the hungry migrants travel north. Just like their Baltimore oriole brethren, orchards have a sweet tooth and drop by backyards with the right spread of fruit and nectar offerings. They're even known to stop at sugar-water feeders.

"One great way to attract orioles is by offering orange halves. Just stick the oranges on a nail and enjoy watching the orioles feast," says Emma Greig, the project leader for Project FeederWatch of the Cornell Lab of Ornithology.

Grape jelly is always an oriole favorite, but serve it in moderation. If you're worried about bugs eating more of the jelly than the birds do, Emma shares a solution: "Try moving jelly feeders around your backyard periodically. Birds will notice them in their new locations more quickly than insects. And remember that insects are good creatures to have in your yard, especially pollinators like bees, so don't despair if they insist on having a small share of the jelly."

For orchard orioles, migration back to their winter homes begins in mid-to-late summer, and even as early as mid-July. This is also when they load up on berries, like ripe mulberries and chokeberries, to help them on their journey south.

FROM LEFT: DANITA DELIMONT/SHUTTERSTOCK; AGAMI PHOTO AGENCY/SHUTTERSTOCK

SIGNATURE LOOK

More bold than females, male orchard orioles sport black head feathers, a burnt orange chest, and a black tail and wings with white accents.

The Most Stellar Jay

Lure bold and witty Steller's jays with their favorite foods to experience their playful antics.

SMART, GREGARIOUS AND handsome, the Steller's jay lives year-round in the western half of North America, often visiting yards, campgrounds and picnic areas.

From a distance, the Steller's, which is related to the blue jay, may look like just a dark crested bird. A closer view reveals its striking dark head and shoulders contrasted with its deep blue body and tail.

Jeff Black, a Department of Wildlife professor at Humboldt State University based in Arcata, California, has been studying Steller's jays since 1998. These brightly colored jays belong to the corvid family, known to be among the most intelligent in the avian world. That, along with the birds' sociable nature, makes it easy to observe them.

"Here in Arcata, California, jay pairs stake claim to our yards, both front and back, and they stay all day and all year," Jeff says. Researchers fit the birds with leg bands, each with a different color combination to identify them.

"Jay pairs readily come to bird feeders, so we can see who's who and who they are hanging out with or chasing off," Jeff says.

To attract Steller's to a feeder, offer peanuts, black oil sunflower seeds, suet or fruit. Pine and oak trees are alluring cover and provide the birds additional food and nesting sites.

Steller's are opportunistic, eating any leftovers people may leave behind, insects, berries, nuts, bird eggs and even small animals such as lizards. As cold weather approaches, they hide food for later retrieval, gathering nuts and seeds into their throats and stuffing the nourishment in nooks and other hiding spots for later in the year.

These clever and social jays communicate in a variety of ways. Jeff says, "They have dozens of calls conveying different information." These include harsh rattles and melodious notes.

"Steller's jays also imitate calls made by hawk species they live with," he says. In winter, they use those calls to scare other birds away from feeders, so all the food is left to them. Using their voices in another way, they team up to scold and chase away predators, including the great horned owl, in a group behavior that ornithologists call mobbing.

Adults likely mate for life. They engage in courtship feeding and show off by throwing their crests and blue feathers around. During breeding season, a pair gathers pine needles, twigs, grasses and mud to construct a cup-shaped nest where the female incubates up to six blue-green eggs with dark brown spots.

Steller's jay

BIRDS OF A DIFFERENT FEATHER

These jays are found in a variety of environments from Alaska to Nicaragua. There are many subspecies, differing mainly in the pattern of white or blue markings on the head.

"Steller's are one of my favorite birds to watch. I love their dusty blue color against the deep green pines in the mountains of New Mexico."

Pat Northington
AUSTIN, TEXAS

FIRST CLASSIFIED

Steller's jays are named after German naturalist Georg Steller. He first documented them on an expedition to an Alaskan island in 1741.

LINGUISTIC TWIST

The tufted titmouse's name may seem a bit odd, but there's an interesting story behind its origin. The second part of the bird's name is actually derived from the Old English word *mase*, meaning "small bird."

"The tufted titmouse is a favorite among photographers. The birds seem to be extra friendly and almost always have cheerful expressions."

John Baughman
FISHERS, INDIANA

Grab-and-Go Masters

Find out why tufted titmice take their dinners and run—and where they go with the food.

THE NEXT TIME you notice a large group of bird species congregating in your backyard, scan the hungry crowd for a stocky, gray-crested bird with a white belly, peach coloring on its flanks and a small black patch on its forehead. The tufted titmouse is a common sight among small winter groupings of chickadees, nuthatches and woodpeckers. It can be spotted year-round in backyards and parks in the eastern half of the U.S.

Although you can attract tufted titmice to your yard in any season, fall and winter are especially good opportunities to set up hanging feeders—that's when the bird's normal prey, insects, become harder to come by.

Tufted titmice love sunflower seeds, but they'll snack on suet and peanuts, too. Instead of staying at the feeder to eat, this bird takes one seed at a time from the feeder, flies away with it and then hammers the shell open with its stout bill. If not yet ready to eat, it will store the shelled seed in a bark crevice or other safe hiding place. The flier doesn't travel far though—most titmice stockpiles are no more than about 130 feet away from a particular feeder.

During warmer months, these small songbirds mainly stick together in lifelong mating pairs within established territories. In spring, the female finds a natural tree cavity, abandoned woodpecker hole or nest box instead of carving out her own place to call home. "Maintaining or encouraging the growth of large trees in your yard is a great way to cultivate a tufted titmouse habitat," says Emma Greig, the project leader for Project FeederWatch of the Cornell Lab of Ornithology. "They really enjoy a deciduous woodland habitat."

Titmouse nests are lined with soft material, such as moss and grass. The bold birds may even steal pieces of fur from live animals for their nests!

For tufted titmice, raising a brood is a family affair, with both male and female birds feeding the young. Once in a while, a juvenile tufted titmouse will actually remain with its parents for the following breeding season to help care for the next generation.

If you're just beginning to learn different birdcalls, the tufted titmouse's bright and clear *peter-peter-peter* whistle is a fantastic one to add to your repertoire. Male tufted titmice often use this song when they're trying to attract a mate and will repeat it multiple times in quick succession.

Tufted titmice go foraging for seeds and insects, particularly caterpillars, in the summer. The birds hop along tree branches as they search for their favorite foods, often acrobatically hanging upside down from heavier branches.

FROM LEFT: JOHN BAUGHMAN; STEVE AND DAVE MASLOWSKI

Forest Dwellers

Be on the lookout for the energy that a banditry of mountain chickadees brings.

CHICKADEES ARE EXTREMELY verbose birds. They sing *fee-bee* when amorous. They scold *chick-a-dee*, adding more *dees* the higher their anxiety. And when the risk is more acute, such as a soaring hawk overhead, they shriek.

"That shriek means 'freeze' to the flock," says Arch McCallum, a retired biology professor and the lead expert on mountain chickadees for the Cornell Lab of Ornithology's Birds of the World.

If you live in the Mountain West, a vocal black, white and gray bird might be a black-capped chickadee or its closest cousin, a mountain chickadee. The two are similar in size, about 4 inches long, with large heads, long tails and small bills. Both have a prominent black cap, white cheeks, light gray to buff sides and a black throat patch, but only mountain chickadees have a white streak above their eyes.

Mountain chickadees lay eggs in woodpecker holes and other cavities that they line with scavenged fur and moss. They use small man-made nest boxes, too. If you hear a hiss coming from a birdhouse, it might actually be a mountain chickadee mimicking the sound of a snake to deter an intruder.

The eggs are dull white with red spots. It takes more than three weeks for the chicks to hatch and fledge. If the adults need to fetch food during that time, they cover the eggs or hatchlings with a fur "blanket" to hide them.

"Mountain chickadees live in impregnable places behind a lot of wood where the young hang out as long as possible because it's safe," Arch says. "When they fly out, it's full-bore. They're really ready!"

A flock of mountain chickadees, called a banditry, is typically up to three mated pairs plus several juveniles. Interestingly, the young birds are usually not the offspring of the pairs in the banditry. The only time mountain chickadees migrate is when they leave their mom and dad to find another flock, though they'll move temporarily downslope during a harsh winter.

Flocks readily come to feeders for sunflower seeds. They approach one at a time, grabbing a seed and carrying it to a nearby branch. Holding the seed with its feet, the bird pokes decisively at the seam until it breaks apart; the bird then eats the nutritious nugget inside or stashes it for a future meal.

"Mountain chickadees cache their finds in the bark and needles of trees and on the ground," Arch says. "I've seen them fly straight to a place under a tree and pull out a seed. They have special memory for where they've put seeds. Their survival depends on it."

These little sprites are full of life and fun to watch, sure to make you smile as they frolic around a feeder.

"Mountain chickadees are quite popular here. I enjoy watching them through my window—I can always tell it's them by their call."

Karlie Larson
SPIRIT LAKE, IDAHO

YEAR-ROUND TUNES

Chickadees are nonmigratory, staying within their ranges all year. A mountain chickadee's buzzy call is distinguished from the black-capped by its harsher tone.

THERE'S NO PLACE LIKE HOME

While black-capped chickadees live in deciduous forests, mountain chickadees prefer to congregate in conifers in western forests from Canada to Texas.

Rare male yellow cardinal

CARDINALS OF ANOTHER COLOR

Rare genetic variations called xanthochroism can cause male cardinals to be yellow instead of the familiar red.

"Cardinals are by far the favorite bird for students on field trips, even beating out our Iowa state bird, the American goldfinch."

Mike Havlik, Naturalist
DALLAS COUNTY CONSERVATION BOARD

Cardinal Rules

Learn how to turn your landscape into a safe haven for this iconic species.

IT'S HARD TO MISS a male cardinal and his bold red feathers, black face mask and spiked crest. Although the female is a bit more subdued, she is no less adored. Either is a go-to critter for holiday cards, in snowy scenes that take on vibrancy thanks to the dash of red.

Despite being fairly common, the birds can be elusive. Cardinals often visit feeders as the sun is setting, when their red feathers are muted under low light conditions. They like to eat from trays or platforms, preferring sunflower and safflower seeds and often roasted, unsalted peanuts. Seeds and nuts are no match for the hefty beaks. Cracked corn is worth setting out, too.

"I'll sprinkle seeds directly on the ground or the sidewalk to give cardinals easy access to a meal," says Mike Havlik, a naturalist for the Dallas County Conservation Board in central Iowa.

A repetitive *pew, pew, pew, pew* song easily reveals the location of cardinals. Females contribute to the backyard concerts, often singing to reinforce pair bonding early in the breeding season. A male's bold red coloration is thought to help attract mates. The brightness is related to diet, and studies indicate that the showier males tend to hold better territories, provide extra parental care and show higher success when it comes to nesting.

Cardinals generally stay in the same area, which helps them get a jump-start on nesting, with some laying eggs by February. This long breeding season allows for multiple broods each year and ensures the survival of at least a few offspring. Cardinals aren't particular when it comes to nest location, and this generalist approach makes them susceptible to predation.

Thick cover provides the most ideal habitat for cardinals in every season. Hedgerows, shrubby stands, overgrown fields and forest edges all make suitable winter roosting sites. Cardinals thrive in towns and suburbs, and the species has expanded northward from its historic range.

While northern cardinals are abundant in the East, Midwest and Southwest, there are some regional variations in the species, especially in the Southwest and Mexico. Some scientists suggest that cardinals in the Sonoran Desert might be a different species from those found elsewhere in the United States, despite their proximity to northern cardinals in other southwestern deserts. Cardinals in the Sonoran Desert are somewhat larger, with longer crests, and the males are paler red. They also have slightly different songs. Regardless of the minute variations, they all look like cardinals when perched on a feeder.

HIM OR HER?

Male and female cardinals are easy to tell apart. Males, like this one, are red all over with black on their faces, while females are brown with red accents.

PEST PATROL

Downies snack on insects that harm trees, like bark beetles and apple borers—so be thankful if you see one hopping on the branches in your yard.

Social Season

When temperatures drop, downy woodpeckers get more active and expand their clique.

ONE OF WINTER'S best sights is watching through a kitchen window as downy woodpeckers flit from suet feeders to nearby trees.

Affectionately called downies, these woodpeckers might easily be mistaken for a nuthatch clinging acrobatically to the side of a feeder or a peppy chickadee, with its bold black-and-white coloring. Look for a bird slightly smaller than a robin with a white belly and back, black wings with white spots and white facial stripes against a mostly black head. Males and females can be told apart by a red marking on the back of the male's head.

Downies reside in most of the United States and Canada, with the exception of the far north and the driest zones in the Southwest. Near the Pacific coast, some downies are muddled-looking—their bright bellies have tan accents, and they have fewer white dots spotting their wings.

These cheery checkered birds have expanded their ranges in the last few years, despite a changing, more urban, environment.

"There has been an expansion," says Kimberly Sullivan, associate professor of biology at Utah State University. "They've done quite well in suburban areas because they visit feeders and don't mind open areas."

They are drawn to feeders in many locations, both developed and rural. Hang one of their favorite treats, suet, to get their attention. Kimberly suggests getting suet scraps from your local butcher and hanging them in a mesh bag along with traditional cage feeders. In warmer months when suet spoils easily, black oil sunflower seeds, millet, peanuts and peanut butter are suitable meals.

Like most woodpeckers, downies use their exceptional long tongues to scavenge. "The very bristly tip of their tongues, almost like a bottle brush, impales and holds onto larvae," says Kimberly.

Downies' small size also gives them another advantage over their fellow woodpeckers. They are adept at climbing up large tree trunks and branches, but they also glean bugs and grubs from weeds, grasses and thin twigs that can support their 1-ounce frames.

In winter, downies are more social, teaming up with kinglets, chickadees and nuthatches to maximize their foraging efforts. "When a mixed flock comes into their territory, they usually join it," Kimberly says. Chickadees are the sentinels of the group and are usually the first to call out a nearby predator. This dynamic allows downies to spend more time digging in through the tree bark and less time on high alert.

Courtship begins toward the end of winter. Both sexes drum on trees (and sometimes unfortunate chimneys) to claim their territory and indicate they're ready to mate. They also call out to each other in whinnying, high-pitched notes that are accented by excited *piks*. Once paired, the partners dig out a cavity in a dead tree for their nest.

LOOK-ALIKES

Hairy woodpeckers (left) have the same coloration but are larger than downies (right). A practiced eye can tell them apart by the size of their beaks, too. The hairy's beak is almost as long as its head, while downies' beaks are shorter, comparatively.

"Feed downies year-round! There's nothing cuter than baby woodpeckers learning to come to the feeder in spring."

Boni Trombetta
WEST CHESTER, PENNSYLVANIA

Hawk Look-Alikes

Learn how to tell the Cooper's and the sharp-shinned apart.

COOPER'S HAWK

HEAD SIZE

Proportional head that's easy to see in flight.

HEAD COLOR

Dark cap with lighter coloring on the neck.

LEGS

Thicker with a shorter appearance.

TAIL

Tail feathers create a rounded look, with middle ones longer than the outer ones.

RANGE

Seen throughout the lower 48 states during most of the year.

SHARP-SHINNED HAWK

HEAD SIZE

Smaller head that barely sticks out when in flight.

HEAD COLOR

Gray beginning on the top of the head and continuing down through the neck feathers.

LEGS

Long and very thin.

TAIL

Tail is more square and uniform.

RANGE

Stays year-round in parts of the Northwest and the Northeast; seen in most of the U.S. during the nonbreeding season.

Large beaks help ravens pick meat off carrion.

With wingspans over a meter, ravens are much larger than crows.

Common ravens have shaggy throat feathers and thick, long necks.

COMMON RAVEN

A slightly pointed tail is one of the most reliable ID marks.

Raven or Crow?

Tips for differentiating these clever cousins in the corvid family.

MORE HELPFUL HINTS

American crows live in most states, but common ravens are found only in the North, Northeast and West. If you're in the Great Plains, Midwest or Southeast, the big black bird you see is probably a crow. Ravens tend to travel solo or with a partner, while crows flock in larger groups. Listen for the raven's low grumbling or a crow's high-pitched caw.

CHAPTER 2

Amazing Hummingbirds

Stunning photos and feeding tips will inspire you to create a haven for these fun-to-watch birds.

Hummingbird Tales

Zip! Zoom! Snap! You have to be quick to capture photos of these teensy birds, but many *Birds & Blooms* readers have been rewarded with memorable moments.

Every summer I try to get to a local preserve frequented by ruby-throated hummingbirds. It's a good place to meet other photographers. A bright and sunny day gave me the assist I needed to catch this lovely little flier.

Robert Kaplan
ROSLYN HEIGHTS, NEW YORK

▲ **I captured this photo** of a female Anna's at a Rockin' Deep Purple salvia bloom. Because I live in the Skagit Valley, I am usually able to photograph Anna's in my backyard all throughout the year.

Jamie Bartram
SEDRO-WOOLLEY, WASHINGTON

► **Hummingbirds** are my favorite birds to photograph. I'm so happy they love the rose of Sharon bush that is outside near my deck.

Karen Smith
NASHVILLE, TENNESSEE

We are lucky enough to have Costa's hummingbirds year-round. This gorgeous male perched outside our kitchen window every day for about two weeks. As if on cue, he would wait for me to come to the window with my camera and then position himself in such a way as to show off his beautiful gorget.

Carla Ritter
IVINS, UTAH

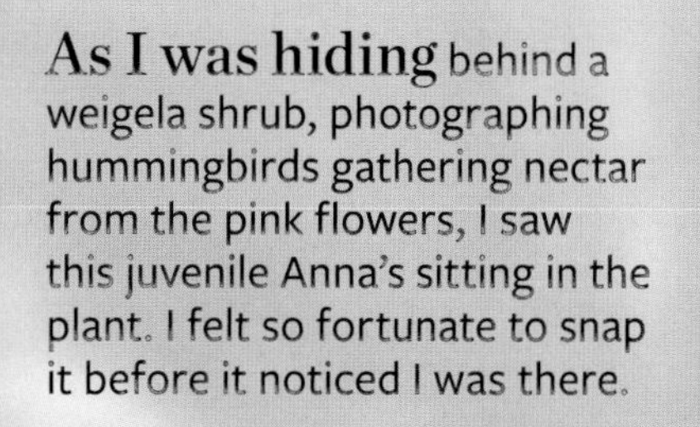

As I was hiding behind a weigela shrub, photographing hummingbirds gathering nectar from the pink flowers, I saw this juvenile Anna's sitting in the plant. I felt so fortunate to snap it before it noticed I was there.

Donna Ruiz
CAMERON PARK, CALIFORNIA

▲ **I took 30 photos** of this beautiful female broad-tailed hummingbird as she sipped nectar from my Cold Hardy Pink salvia. I am blessed to see these flying jewels from about mid-July to the first week of October each year.

Linda Minns
GOODWELL, OKLAHOMA

◄ **A female broad-tailed** hummingbird nested in the same place in our front yard for three years. I was afforded a unique opportunity to watch and observe from our window as this female raised her young.

Carol Galloway
CENTENNIAL, COLORADO

This photograph was taken in Balboa Park in San Diego, California. The park has an extensive series of gardens that attract a large number of hummingbirds, as well as many other pollinators. While walking the gardens early one spring morning, I came upon this Allen's hummingbird. These birds usually catch one's attention as they quickly move from flower to flower feeding on nectar, but this one was enjoying a quiet moment. He seemed to be pausing to take in the beauty that surrounded him.

Stuart Allison
CORONADO, CALIFORNIA

◀ **This Rufous** hummingbird aggressively guarded the feeder we had just put out and wouldn't let any other hummers come to it. But he sure was a joy to watch, with his brilliant orange gorget shining in the sunlight.

Deborah Whiting
MIDLAND, TEXAS

▼ **I'd been trying** to get a picture of a hummingbird (any hummingbird!) sitting on a branch with a nice background for a very long time. I was really excited when this male broad-billed hummingbird perched close to me.

Jane Miller
TUCSON, ARIZONA

Some of my best photos are taken right in my backyard. I plant perennials and annuals that specifically draw in the birds and bees. I love this action shot of a female ruby-throated hummingbird.

Jenny Miner
IRMA, WISCONSIN

As I was getting ready to go to work, a friend called me and told me that he knew where a white ruby-throated hummingbird was spotted in a neighboring county. It turned out to be almost completely leucistic, making it even more special!

Kenny Nations
HEBER SPRINGS, ARKANSAS

▲ **While I was sitting** in my sunroom, a beautiful ruby-throated hummingbird perched on a limb of a nearby hemlock tree. Luckily, my camera was next to me with a telephoto lens mounted and I was able to get many wonderful shots of this bird.

Steven Deam
FORT WAYNE, INDIANA

◀ **I went to Costa Rica,** where there are now around 60 hummingbird species, and I saw more than a dozen during my trip. These two are green-crowned brilliants. I've since traveled to Ecuador and Panama to photograph even more.

Paul Lawson
NEW CARLISLE, INDIANA

Black-bellied hummingbird photographed in Costa Rica by Elijah Gildea

Shutterbug Magic

Four *Birds & Blooms* readers share their tips for spectacular hummingbird photos.

Anna's hummingbird by Elijah Gildea

Elijah Gildea

REDDING, CALIFORNIA
EQUIPMENT: NIKON D850, NIKON 200-500 LENS

IN 2006, Elijah spotted a pair of bald eagles—the first he'd seen in his life. He was so excited that he went out the next day and purchased a new camera. Soon he was photographing rufous hummingbirds nearby, then traveling to find even more species. "I am always in pursuit of capturing incredible or beautiful hummingbird moments," he says.

"Hummingbirds caught my eye because of their iridescent colors, and they have kept my interest because of their incredible variety," Elijah says.

His hobby is now a part-time job. He shoots professionally for Perky-Pet bird feeders and leads tours in Costa Rica, while teaching local photography workshops.

In his own backyard, Elijah regularly welcomes six species. "I live on the outskirts of town, which is a great location for hummingbirds," he says. "I have 12 large feeders and spend my mornings drinking coffee, cleaning and refilling feeders, and watching the dozens of hummingbirds." His camera is always close by, no doubt!

ELIJAH'S TOP TIP

Learn the sounds hummingbirds make so it's easier to spot them. Try shooting them while they're perched and still to get sharp, colorful photos.

Bill Friggle

DENVER, PENNSYLVANIA
EQUIPMENT: NIKON D600, NIKON 200-500 LENS

WHEN BILL'S arthritis forced him into a power chair, he felt depressed by his limitations. Reading about a fellow photographer who had similar challenges inspired him to return to the hobby of his youth. "On the days you can, you go out and do what you can," he says.

A longtime shutterbug, Bill started photographing birds only about 10 years ago. *I love birds,* he remembers thinking to himself. *Why am I not photographing them?*

Bill regularly heads to a nearby wildlife management area full of flowers, feeders and the feathered treasures he understands so well.

"Know the hummingbirds," he says. "What are their habits? That allows you to predict where they will be and lets you prefocus your camera on that spot."

Bill enjoys sharing his photos with others, especially his two granddaughters. "I have a screen saver made up of pictures I've taken," he says. "They love to watch it with me, asking about every bird." It seems that inspiring a love of nature in others is another wonderful aspect of Bill's photos.

BILL'S TOP TIP

Patience! Bring a chair, be quiet and wait. Wear the same colors each time you shoot so you blend into the background.

Ruby-throated hummingbird at bee balm by Bill Friggle

Mike Bond

SUMTER, SOUTH CAROLINA
EQUIPMENT: CANON EOS 5D MARK III WITH CUSTOM WHEELCHAIR MOUNT

MIKE BEGAN DABBLING in wildlife photography back in 2007, focusing first on flowers to master camera settings and good composition. He transitioned from flowers to butterflies and then hummingbirds. "I love that moment when your heart rate changes because you've caught something special," Mike says.

The challenges of partial paralysis make his photos all the more impressive. "I can't use my left hand or leg, and I'm confined to a power wheelchair, but I'm not complaining," he says. Instead, Mike used his engineering skills to design a special wheelchair camera mount he calls the C4 Freedom, with a shutter adapter he clicks with his mouth. And the stunning results speak for themselves.

"Have I had milestones and hurdles to overcome?" Mike asks. "Absolutely." But as he points out, "If I can do it, you can, too." He calls what has happened to him The Willchair Effect. "The ultimate reward is to have viewers in awe as they view a moment they'll never see with the naked eye," Mike says. It's a goal he achieves with each spectacular photo.

MIKE'S TOP TIP

Grow a large variety of flowers in your garden to create better, more colorful backgrounds. In the wild, position yourself to catch a hummingbird on a blossom's edge.

Ruby-throated hummingbird at hibiscus by Mike Bond

Anna's hummingbird by Leslie Scopes Anderson

Leslie Scopes Anderson

ARCATA, CALIFORNIA
EQUIPMENT: NIKON D4S, NIKKOR 200-400 LENS

A LIFELONG NATURE LOVER, Leslie first picked up photography as a hobby 60 years ago when her dad gave her a camera at age 12. Over the decades, she's discovered the pleasures of hummingbird photography. "Hummingbirds are the jewels of the animal kingdom," Leslie says. "Working with them involves beautiful flowers, which also adds to the experience."

To overcome the challenge of hummingbirds' quick, darting flights, Leslie waits for them to hover before clicking the shutter repeatedly. "Shoot, shoot, shoot!" she says. "The more frames the merrier." She also recommends trying to focus on their eyes.

Now retired after 30 years of working in graphic design, Leslie lives in the Pacific Northwest and spends time snapping hummers in her favorite spot: her flower-filled backyard. Trips to places like Costa Rica provide opportunities for her to capture new species, such as the gorgeous green-breasted mango hummingbird, which is a personal favorite. "These flying jewels are a symbol for joy!" Leslie says. Her photos certainly prove her point.

LESLIE'S TOP TIP

As photographers like to say, "Point your shadow at it." Keep the sun behind you for maximum color rendition.

Totally Tubular

Plant these flowers and watch hummingbirds flock.

STANDING TALL
Larkspur reaches 2 to 6 feet tall. It looks best when planted in cottage gardens, borders, meadows and natural areas.

1 Larkspur

DELPHINIUM SPP., ZONES 3 TO 7

Although it's a bit picky, larkspur is well worth the effort when spires of blue flowers reach for the sky. Delphiniums require full sun and organic, moist, well-draining soil. Avoid planting it in windy locations, and cut it back around midsummer for a second set of flowers.

Why we love it: *Delphinium exaltatum* is native in the East and sturdy enough to be grown in Zones 4 to 8.

2 Flowering tobacco

NICOTIANA ALATA, ANNUAL

Plant flowering tobacco along sidewalks, next to your deck or patio, or near open windows where you can enjoy the lovely evening fragrance. This adaptable plant reseeds readily and grows best in full sun and rich soils. It also comes in a variety of colors and sizes.

Why we love it: The trumpet-shaped flowers and bold leaves make it a standout in containers and garden beds.

3 Virginia bluebells

MERTENSIA VIRGINICA, ZONES 3 TO 9

Add some blue to those shady spots with this vigorous eastern native. Grow in moist, rich soil and combine with daffodils for a striking spring display. Add hostas and other shade-loving perennials to mask the fading foliage later in the season.

Why we love it: Hummingbirds, bumblebees and other beneficial pollinators appreciate this early source of nectar.

4 Wild petunia

RUELLIA HUMILIS, ZONES 4 TO 8

Each blue flower lasts only one day but is quickly replaced, creating season-long color. A petunia reseeds readily, so plant it where it is able to weave through and commingle with neighboring plants, or deadhead it to prevent reseeding. Grow this 12-inch-tall plant in full sun or a spot with late-afternoon shade.

Why we love it: It's deer and rabbit resistant and adaptable to dry and wet soil.

2, 3: BALL HORTICULTURAL COMPANY; 4: THANAPOL SAMATTAKARN/GETTY IMAGES

5 Indian pink

SPIGELIA MARILANDICA, ZONES 4 TO 8

Often overlooked, this greater southeastern native is considered a hummingbird favorite by gardeners who have grown the colorful plant. It flowers in late spring to early summer and does best in gardens with moist soil and light shade to part sun.

Why we love it: The vibrant red-and-yellow flowers of Little Redhead are sure to increase this plant's popularity and availability at stores.

6 Tall verbena

VERBENA BONARIENSIS, ZONES 7 TO 11

Watch as hummingbirds and butterflies flock to this beauty that grows up to 4 feet tall. Grow in full to part sun for the best season-long displays. It reseeds readily for repeat appearances and can be invasive in parts of the Southeast, Northwest and western U.S.

Why we love it: Use as a thriller in containers, allowing it to weave over the edge of the pot and through other plants to extend the bloom time.

7 Crocosmia

CROCOSMIA SPP., ZONES 5 TO 9

Ignite your summer garden with long graceful sprays of brilliant orange-red flowers. Grow in full sun and moist soil. Northern gardeners can dig up the corms in fall and overwinter them in a cool, dark indoor location.

Why we love it: Lucifer's deep orange-red flowers top 4-foot-tall plants for dazzling focal points.

Rufous hummingbird

8 Cape fuchsia

PHYGELIUS CAPENSIS, ZONES 6 TO 10

Give this upright, shrubby plant room to grow and to show off its floral display. It reaches 3 to 5 feet tall and wide, sporting red tubular flowers held in 12- to 18-inch clusters. Enjoy the beauty of these fuchsia-hued flowers in locations with full sun and moist soil.

Why we love it: The flowers of this hardy perennial consistently bring in hummingbirds summer through fall.

9 Red-hot poker

KNIPHOFIA HYBRIDS, ZONES 5 TO 9

Keep this sun-loving perennial happy with well-draining soil, and clusters of red, orange, cream or white flowers will appear and delight in summer. They make fantastic cut flowers, but you'll want to leave plenty of blooms for the hummingbirds, bees and butterflies to enjoy.

Why we love it: You need only a few plants to make an absolutely stunning display.

10 Firecracker plant

CUPHEA SPP., ZONES 8 TO 11

Draw hummingbirds and butterflies to your back door with pots of cuphea. It comes in a range of hues, but flowers are usually tipped in red, yellow or white, resembling a lit cigar or firecracker. This 12- to 24-inch-tall plant flowers freely all summer; no deadheading needed.

Why we love it: Bat face (*Cuphea llavea*) has unique flowers that both kids and hummingbirds adore.

Bird Supermoms

Female hummingbirds amaze with incredible maternal skills.

Black-chinned hummingbird

Ruby-throated hummingbird feeding nestlings

EVERYONE KNOWS of male hummingbirds and their dazzling iridescent hues. But the females wow us in a more practical way: They are among the best mothers in the bird world. Male hummingbirds take no part in raising the young, so these miniature moms do the big job all by themselves.

A Perfect Cradle

To shelter her cherished eggs, a female hummingbird builds an exquisite nest that is equally as precious as it is practical. She fashions a tiny cup from the finest plant materials, like the wispy down from dandelions or thistles, and places it on top of a branch, tying them together with sticky spiderwebs. She covers the outside of the nest with tiny flakes of lichen to camouflage her masterpiece.

The build time is anywhere from a week to 10 days, and the resulting nest looks just like a bump on a branch—almost impossible to spot.

Egg-Cellent Care

Once her nest is complete, the female lays two eggs (sometimes only one), each roughly the size of a bean. When incubation starts, she strikes a balance between keeping the eggs warm and keeping herself alive—hummingbirds burn a lot of energy, even when they're sitting still, so the female leaves the nest frequently to find food for herself. During the day, she'll usually leave five or six times per hour, spending a few minutes grabbing a meal before returning to settle on the eggs again. In all, she manages to keep the eggs covered for about three-quarters of daylight and the entire night.

The weather affects the length of the incubation period. If it's warm and food is easy to find, the female spends more time on the eggs and they may hatch in as little as 12 days. If it's cold and wet or if the female has to take longer feeding trips, extending the time she's away from her eggs, they may take up to 19 days to hatch. But the tenacious mother keeps on incubating, no matter how long it takes.

Growing Up

After the eggs hatch, the little supermom switches to an even higher gear to keep her youngsters warm and fed. Scrawny and naked, the babies look like little space aliens at first. The female needs to spend nearly every minute caring for them when she's not zipping away to get food.

Leaving the nest only for brief foraging forays, the female speeds away to gather up nectar, pollen and tiny insects. She feeds these items to the young in a slurry form, jabbing her bill far down the throat of each nestling to transfer the nutritious liquid lunch. Never fear, she won't impale her babies with that long bill.

The young soon start to sprout feathers. Within two weeks they may sit on the rim of the nest and start to stretch their wings. About three weeks after hatching, they make their perilous first flights, whirring away from the nest.

After the young start flying, the female continues to monitor and feed them for another week. You may think she deserves a rest, but she's probably hard at work building a different nest for the second brood while she's still feeding young from the first. It's just another reason why hummingbird mothers are so amazing and hardworking!

KING OF THE HILL

Male broad-tailed hummingbirds, like this one, sit on high perches, ready to chase unwelcome visitors away from their territory.

The Mountain Hummingbird

Listen and look for broad-taileds in their high-elevation habitats.

HUMMINGBIRDS aren't known for the noises they make—unless it's the sound of one zooming past—but broad-tailed hummingbirds are loud visitors.

Female broad-taileds keep up a constant vocal twittering, and males add a loud trill from their specialized wing feathers while in flight. "Once you learn their sound, you won't forget it!" says David Mehlman, who served as director of the Nature Conservancy's Migratory Bird Program.

"The male broad-tailed is the most distinctive-sounding of all North American hummingbirds," David says. If you live in the mountains of the West or visit the region in summer, you're bound to hear these very common and abundant hummingbirds, maybe even before you see them.

Aside from the noise, it is the male's bold throat that first catches attention, not the tail. An adult male sports a showy rose-magenta patch on the throat called a gorget. It's a bright contrast to the tail, which is slightly wider and longer than that of most other hummingbirds found in the U.S. and Canada, extending beyond the wingtips when the bird is perched and resting. Both male and female have a green back and crown and a white chest. The female has rusty sides and white tips on the outer tail feathers.

The plentiful nectar of alpine meadow wildflowers draws crowds of broad-tailed hummingbirds to the Rockies, Sierras, Guadalupes and other ranges, spanning from Texas to Montana. Insects and tree sap round out their regular menu of high-elevation blooms.

Even in the mountain breeding grounds, broad-tailed hummers don't form pair bonds. Females sometimes outnumber males, but with no pair bonds, males may mate with several females. Males tend to perch on high vantage points near feeders, keeping a lookout for other males, while crowds of females and, later in the season, juveniles swarm the feeders from dawn to dusk.

During migration to and from Mexico, broad-taileds turn up at lower elevations, sometimes even visiting cities. David's home in New Mexico is about a mile above sea level, but broad-taileds visit only when passing through. "If I want to see them in summer, I have to head up to 8,000 or 9,000 feet," he says.

Gardeners who live in the mountains or in the migration path of broad-taileds can attract these fliers with the usual suite of flowers, such as penstemon, red hot poker, trumpet honeysuckle, salvia and bee balm, all of which add colorful flair to yards. Keep an eye—and an ear—out for these hummers as they make your backyard a regular stop.

Broad-tailed hummingbird

FEED A MULTITUDE

Hang a few feeders instead of one because these territorial birds come in droves.

EXPANDING EAST

Several types of western hummingbirds, including broad-taileds, are now showing up in the Gulf States in fall and winter. While no one knows exactly why, David Mehlman jokes, "Maybe it's the gumbo."

FAVORITE NATIVE

The red birds in a tree shrub (*Scrophularia macrantha*, Zones 4 to 9) attracts broad-tailed hummingbirds where it grows wild in the Southwest. It produces nectar-filled flowers that look just like little birds.

Eastern Gems

Find out why ruby-throated hummingbirds are tiny marvels.

1,200

When ruby-throats are really exerting themselves, their hearts race around 1,200 beats per minute. In calmer times, that rate drops to 600 beats per minute. Humans, in comparison, have a resting heart rate of about 72.

3 Invite these teeny delights into your yard with flowers in their three favorite colors: red, orange and pink.

53 Zipping around in every direction (even backward), the nimble ruby-throated hummingbird beats its wings around 53 times per second.

2 Ruby-throats can consume up to twice their body weight (which is less than a penny) in nectar, small insects and tree sap every day.

25 These little creatures fly about 25 miles per hour and zoom even faster when the wind pushes them along.

500

Some ruby-throats fly nonstop 500 miles across the Gulf of Mexico during migration.

34,000,000

Among the most common and successful hummers, ruby-throats are found during summer across most of the eastern U.S. and east of the Rockies in southern Canada. Their population totals an estimated 34 million birds.

Easy Way to Keep Feeders Clean

Birds & Blooms readers share tried-and-true tips to keep sugar water safe for their favorite hummingbird fliers.

I have several feeders so that I can swap them out for cleaning. I soak them in bleach and water to get the black residue off. Then I use Q-tips to scrub the holes and small nooks. Rinse thoroughly!

Lu-Ann Tucker
WAREHAM, MASSACHUSETTS

Wash with very warm water and scrub with a toothbrush.

Emily Eigenbrode
FREDERICK, MARYLAND

Feeders are easier to keep clean if they are hung in the shade. Mold growth slows significantly.

Barbara Cameron
COGAN STATION, PENNSYLVANIA

I clean hummingbird feeders every three days, especially in hot humid weather, using hot water, a natural cleaner and a special bent brush for hard-to-reach places.

Gayla Metzger
BATTLE CREEK, MICHIGAN

Scrub the feeder with a brush and then fill with a hot water and vinegar mixture. Let it soak, rinse well and then air dry before filling.

Cher Loskota
MOUNTAIN HOME, ARKANSAS

I put ¼ cup rice and ½ cup hot water in a feeder and shake it. The rice is abrasive, so it cleans the inside of the feeder.

Kerry Rose
VALLEYFORD, WASHINGTON

CHAPTER 3

Birds In-Depth

Take a close look at birdlife and beautiful species found beyond the backyard.

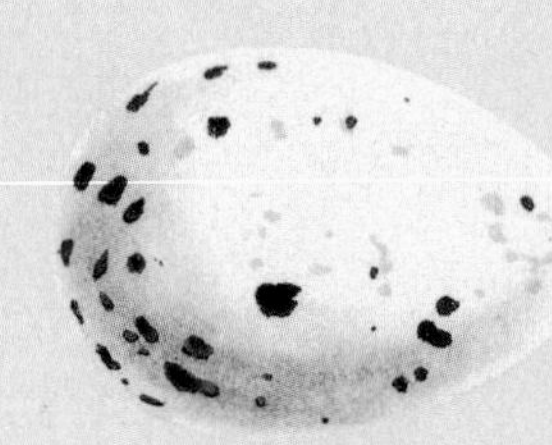

What's Hatching?

Dive into the world of eggs and explore how parenthood starts well before the first shell cracks.

BIRD EGGS RANGE IN COLOR and can be ornately maculated with spots, blotches and scrawls. They vary in shape and size, and they must be thick enough to withstand the weight of an incubating parent but thin enough to allow the embryo to break through and hatch. Other than heat and protection, all the resources needed for a chick to grow and mature are packaged cleanly and tightly in the eggshell surrounding it. Discover how egg color, size and incubation change from species to species.

RUBY-THROATED HUMMINGBIRD

A kiwi lays the largest egg in relation to its body size, but hummingbirds come in a close second when you add up the total volume of the two eggs laid in each clutch. Nests are built and eggs are incubated by the females. Like all hummingbirds, the ruby-throated species lays immaculate white eggs, but the eggs sit so deep in the cup-shaped nest that a predator doesn't see them unless it is directly above the nest.

AMERICAN ROBIN

Spotless, bright blue-green eggs in the American robin's mud-lined nest are a sure sign that spring has arrived in North America—and sometimes they appear before the season itself. In places where trees are very sparse, robins may nest on the ground. Many eggs don't make it to hatching because of the diverse predators, including squirrels, snakes and crows, that easily rob the robin clutch. In response to adversity, robins quickly build their nests again, but the later clutches might contain fewer eggs.

BLUE JAY

Blue jays swiftly remove sharp eggshell fragments to protect their newly hatched brood from harm. Discarding shells also helps prevent both microbial infestations and pungent-smelling cues that might alert nest predators about the location of the clutch. In this jay's family, only the female incubates the eggs, but both parents work to provision the hungry chicks upon hatching.

YELLOW WARBLER

Yellow warblers are popular targets of brood parasitic brown-headed cowbirds. When both species' eggs are present in a nest, the warbler eggs often fail to hatch or the chicks might not make it to fledging. When cowbirds are near the nest, yellow warblers emit alarm calls and the female may sit on the nest with wings spread out to keep other birds at bay. If the warblers find a cowbird egg in their nest, they may bury it by building a new layer of nest on top of the intruder's egg.

BLACK-CAPPED CHICKADEE

The eggs of these cavity-nesting birds are rarely seen by most birders because the species does not usually choose artificial nest boxes. Instead, they prefer to breed in old woodpecker holes or in holes of rotting stumps. There is a trade-off, though. Because woodpecker holes are safer, competition with other cavity-nesting birds for the holes is fiercer. Many embryos of chickadees are sired by males other than the social father, a phenomenon known as extra-pair paternity.

4 AMAZING EGG FACTS

1. Despite the broad variety in colors and markings displayed by bird eggs, just two pigments are responsible for staining the shells of all known species of living and extinct birds, including dinosaurs.

2. An egg that is pear-shaped easily settles within the nest or even on bare ground if the parents opt not to build a nest.

3. Eggshell colors serve to signal the identity of each egg. For example, a parasitic brown-headed cowbird egg sticks out in the nest among an American robin's blue eggs. Typically, the robin recognizes the cowbird egg and tosses it out.

4. The eggshell serves as a calcium supply for the growing embryo inside. As the embryo matures, the shell slowly becomes thinner and the hatchling has an easier time breaking through.

CEDAR WAXWING

Erratic in their distribution and where they breed, cedar waxwings time their egg laying with late-ripening fruit. The waxwing egg is a balance of a pale bluish gray and a suite of darker, delicate spotting patterns. With a tight pair bond, both parents build the nest, incubate the eggs and, once the eggs hatch, feed the nestlings a mostly fruit diet.

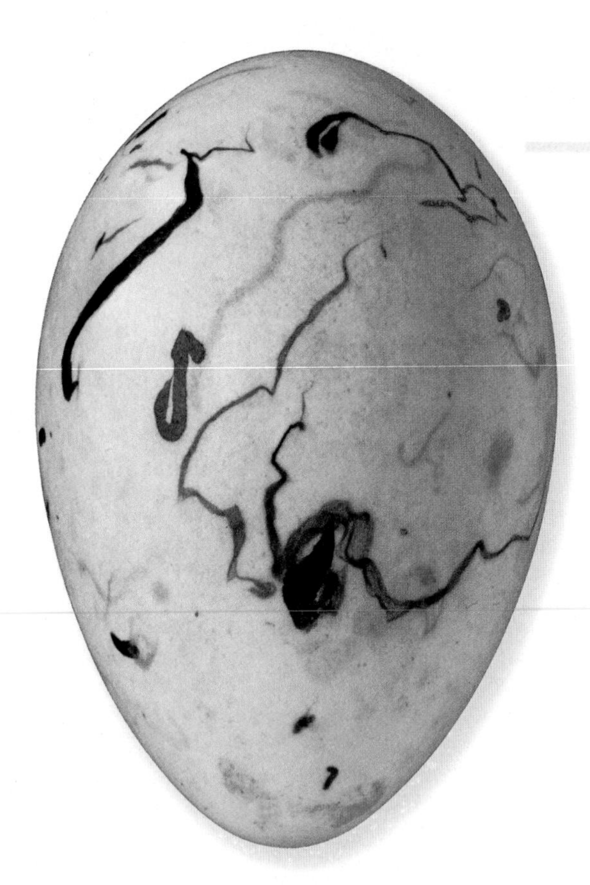

ACTUAL SIZE

CLUTCH SIZE: 3 TO 7 EGGS

BALTIMORE ORIOLE

The pale gray-blue oriole egg is covered with sparsely distributed lines and squiggles that marble the egg. Occasionally, a nest may be attended by two birds that look like females. But usually one of them is actually a young male breeding for the first time, still displaying cryptic plumage that allows it to stay under the radar of older and more competitive males.

ACTUAL SIZE

CLUTCH SIZE: 1 TO 4 EGGS

OSPREY

It takes an osprey five weeks or so to complete the incubation period for its dark blotch-covered eggs. Older birds often pair with previous partners, reusing and improving the preceding year's nest to build an even bulkier and presumably safer site for incubating their eggs. Ospreys sometimes nest in loose colonies, where they observe and copy cues from their neighbors, particularly about the location those neighbors made their latest catch to feed their young.

NORTHERN CARDINAL

The beige base color and brown spots of the cardinal's egg sharply contrast with the bright red plumage of the male parent. Perhaps because the female has a mix of more subdued reddish brown plumage, she is the sex responsible for incubating the eggs. She also builds the delicate nest, constructing the base by crushing twigs with her powerful beak. All the while, she's followed and fed by the male as part of his nuptial feedings.

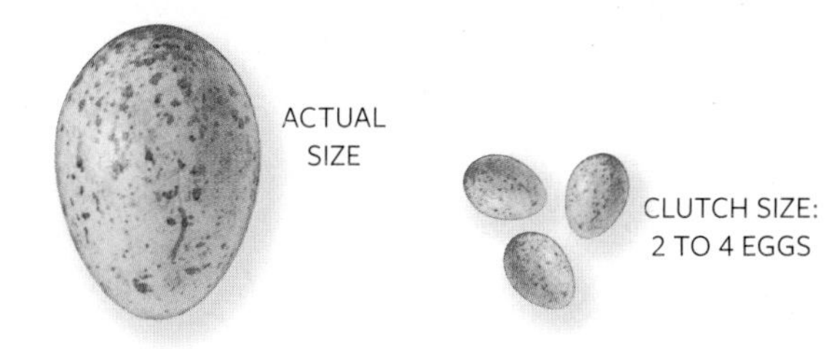

ACTUAL SIZE

SANDHILL CRANE

These cranes lay one to three relatively small eggs that are pale brown and marked with reddish brown blotches for camouflage. Both parents attend the nest and spend about a month taking turns incubating the eggs, but this is just a small part of their parental duties. They spend the next nine months looking after the young until they are independent. Sandhill cranes also make good foster parents—despite the variability in eggs, they don't recognize their own and accept other eggs.

Cognitive Capabilities

Think your feathered friends lack smarts? Think again!

Rose-breasted grosbeaks may remember where feeders are located in their territory.

FROM LEFT: STEVEN SHARP PHOTOGRAPHY/GETTY IMAGES; CHRISTINE HAINES

Watch mountain chickadees flit back and forth to feeders, collecting extra seeds for winter.

NATURE LOVERS have a fondness for their backyard birds—one that is often reserved for dogs, cats and other pets—even though these friends tend to come and go with the seasons. Turns out, birds are more like pets than you think, as the same ones often show up at the same feeders year after year.

"People really underestimate the cognitive abilities of animals in general, which is their ability to perceive, integrate and use information," says Carrie Branch, a postdoctoral fellow at the Cornell Lab of Ornithology. She studies communication and cognition in birds, with a special emphasis on chickadees. "They learn. And to learn, you have to remember things. They learn from their experiences and remember just like people do."

MAKING MEMORIES THAT LAST

Memory duration varies from bird to bird. "There's evidence, depending on the bird, of course, that they remember variations of certain songs or locations for up to two years," Carrie says. "They definitely have long-term memory."

INSTINCT AND MEMORY DIFFER

Think about migratory birds and how they return to the same region year after year. That's instinctual. It involves natural smarts, but not necessarily learning. By contrast, think about how birds know where feeders are located. "They couldn't possibly instinctively know that a feeder exists in someone's yard," Carrie says. "They would have to find it and remember that it exists to come back to it."

KEEPING A CACHE

Some resident species, such as titmice, woodpeckers, chickadees and jays, skip migration. Instead, they cache thousands of seeds, storing them throughout their territory. As a part of that process, these birds identify which feeder has their preferred foods and they return to it.

In addition, there's evidence—found by Vladimir Pravosudov, a professor at University of Nevada, Reno—indicating that mountain chickadees, birds that live in harsh conditions at high elevations, have better memory than others. It's because memory is more critical for them to survive.

SKULL SIZE DOESN'T ALWAYS MATTER

Chickadees and other songbirds typically have large brain-to-body ratios. Several studies have found that birds with relatively larger brains tend to be better at adapting to new situations and performing complex tasks.

Could that mean the bigger the bird, the bigger the brain and, therefore, the smarter the bird? "That's actually a controversial topic," Carrie says. "Some large birds are actually not very smart. Looking at specialized regions seems to be more important than overall brain size." That means even smaller birds, like the warbler or hummingbird at your feeders, may be able to display surprising mental abilities.

PERCH PROTECTION

Long-billed hermits are a type of tropical hummingbird, and to attract mates, dominant males claim a perch and incessantly sing. When forced to refuel, they tap into their memories and head straight for flowers full of nectar. Then they quickly return to their perch, making sure it doesn't get snatched.

Safe and Sound Underground

From crannies in coastal rocks to tunnels in Florida subdivisions, dig into the secrets of burrowers.

A tufted puffin in breeding plumage flies into its nest, which is burrowed into a coastal cliff.

BIRDS CREATE AN AMAZING variety of nests to shelter their eggs and young. Some construct massive platforms of sticks in tall trees, others weave intricate cups of plant stems hidden in shrubs or vines, and a few lay eggs inside holes in trees or on a smoothed-over pile of beach sand. But the best-protected and most unusual nests are those placed in subterranean burrows. Meet the birds that have adopted this underground strategy.

Kingfishers

With hefty beaks, shaggy crests and rattling cries, belted kingfishers are commonly spotted around lakes and rivers across North America. Hardly anyone, though, sees the tucked-away nests where they lay their eggs.

Each pair of kingfishers finds a vertical dirt bank, often a high riverbank, and they take turns boring a horizontal tunnel. Loosening the soil with their sharp beaks and shuffling dirt back with their feet, they may dig for a week or more. The finished nook is usually 3 to 6 feet long, but sometimes more than 14 feet. A large chamber sits at the end of the narrow round tunnel. In this secure shelter, parents incubate five to eight eggs for about three weeks and feed the growing nestlings for another four weeks. At that point, the young kingfishers are ready to come out of the burrow and learn to fly.

Although the belted is the only widespread kingfisher in the United States, two others live close to the Mexican border. The green kingfisher is a tiny bird, smaller than a robin but with an enormous beak, while the ringed kingfisher is a bruiser, larger than the belted. They all share the family habit of building nests in dirt banks.

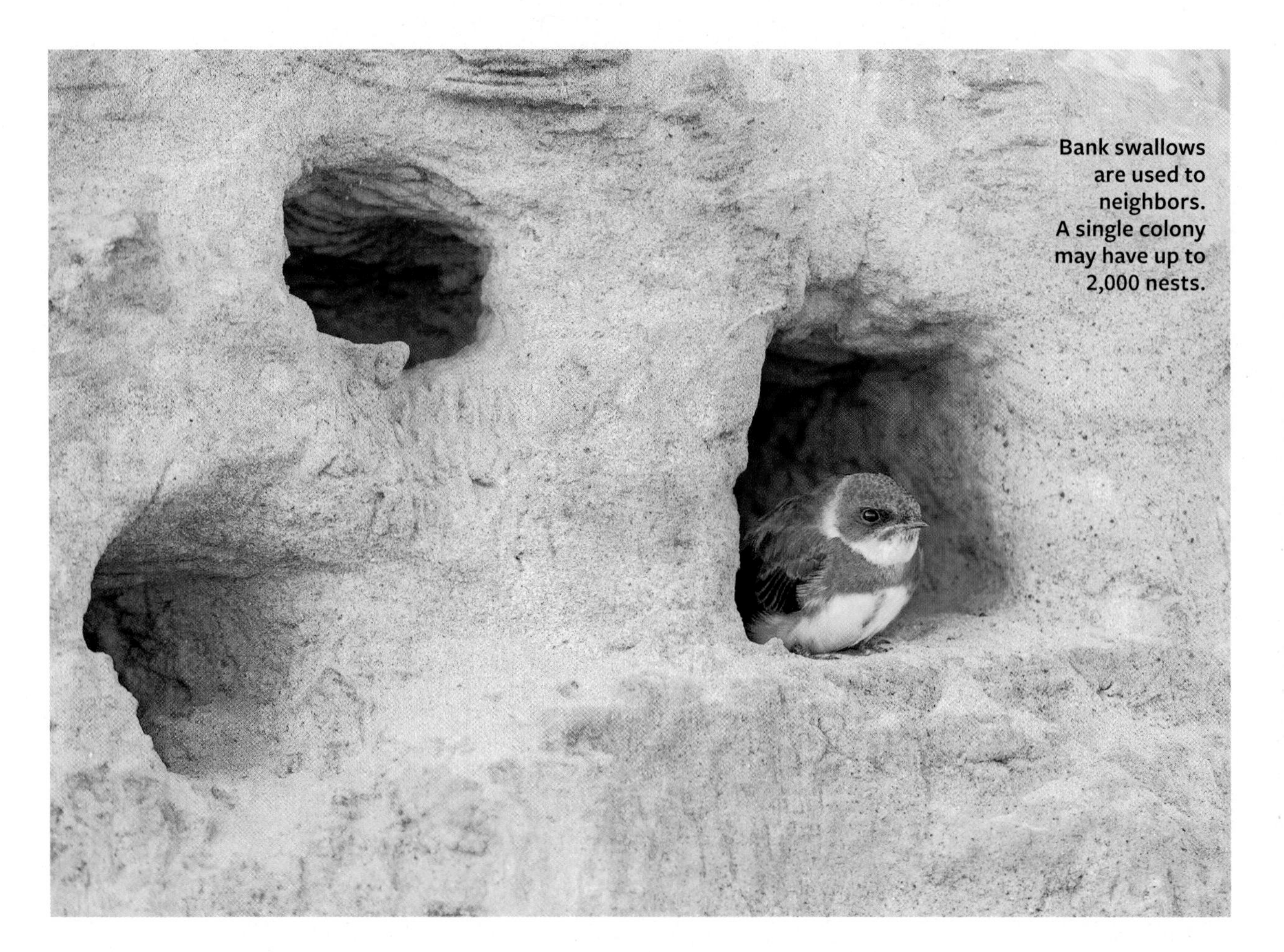

Bank swallows are used to neighbors. A single colony may have up to 2,000 nests.

PREVIOUS SPREAD AND THIS SPREAD, LEFT: BRIAN ZWIEBEL; RIGHT: STEVE AND DAVE MASLOWSKI

Belted kingfishers, like this female, often perch near the banks of rivers, ponds and other bodies of water, where they also nest.

OWL LORE

An old western nickname for the burrowing owl is "howdy owl," because it appears to nod its head as a way of saying hello. Cowboys had many legends about these birds, including that the owls, prairie dogs and rattlesnakes lived together peacefully in the same burrow. They don't, of course. But here are the facts behind the myth: When they're disturbed, young burrowing owls make a harsh buzz that sounds very much like the rattle of a snake. Hearing that sound from deep in a burrow may be enough to make humans (and other animals) stay away.

Swallows

Many swallow homes are out in the open. Barn swallows, of course, build nests in barns, on porches and in sheds, using stiff, dried mud as a foundation. A couple of types of swallows interact with mud and dirt in other ways.

Bank swallows and northern rough-winged swallows are common from coast to coast in summer, and both nest in holes. Bank swallows create tunnels in steep dirt riverbanks, where they seem to love company. On high banks, the lairs of dozens of birds—sometimes a thousand pairs or more—may crowd together, entrances only inches apart. Horizontal tunnels average about 2 feet long, and some bank swallows dig up to 5 feet into the soil—that's quite a feat considering these are the smallest swallows, with bodies less than 5 inches long.

Northern rough-winged swallows are not nearly as sociable, living in very small groups or as isolated pairs. Unlike their hardworking cousins, they usually don't make their burrows; instead, they find holes abandoned by rodents, kingfishers or other creatures, or they move into vacant digs at the edge of a bank swallow colony.

Burrowing Owls

Named for their distinct below-ground habits, burrowing owls scuttle over open prairie and desert floors in the western states and Florida. They're active by day, making them easier to watch than most owls. In the western states, the owls usually dwell in prairie dog colonies, where they take over abandoned quarters. In Florida, many burrowing owls live in vacant lots in towns, and some communities proudly adopt and protect local colonies. Unlike their western cousins, the Florida owls regularly excavate their own homes. A pair may dig a tunnel 10 feet long in two days.

Above: A northern rough-winged swallow is right at home on a steep, rocky bank.

Left: A family of burrowing owls peeks over a dirt mound. Their nest is hidden below.

Wilson's storm-petrels are usually spotted along coastlines, skimming the water.

Seabirds

The most mysterious burrowers are found among the true seabirds. Many of these ocean dwellers raise their young on islands, and the smaller species often excavate burrows or find hollows buried deep among the rocks. Hidden away, the homes are safe from large gulls and other predators.

This secretive behavior seems fitting for storm-petrels, little dark seabirds that flutter low over the waves. They come and go from their nests only at night. Islands off both the Atlantic and Pacific coasts have thousands of nesting pairs. Visit the Farallon Islands near San Francisco during the day, for example, and you'd never guess how many of these secretive birds are concealed underground.

On the other hand, puffins, which are also ground burrowers, are famous even among people who have never seen one in the wild. With their upright posture and colorful beaks, puffins are pictured on signs and T-shirts in coastal communities in Maine and Alaska. They seem flashy, but when it's time to choose a nest site, they go below ground—digging or finding a deep crevice among the rocks. It's just one more example of the ways birds can be endlessly surprising.

During breeding season, Atlantic puffins assemble colonies and build nests in close proximity.

Golden eagle

American Eagles

Bald eagle

Get to know two of North America's largest and most magnificent birds of prey that share a name but little else.

DAVE WELLING (2)

IT'S AN AWE-INSPIRING experience to look up and see a bald eagle or a golden eagle soaring overhead. With similar names and resemblance in their younger life stages, it's natural to assume that they are closely related. But aside from the fact that they both belong to the hawk family, these two eagle species are very distant relatives and have extremely different lifestyles.

Two Groups of Eagles

On a global scale, the name eagle is applied to more than 60 members of the hawk family. They're a diverse selection, mostly large to medium in size, but not necessarily related. The two North American eagles represent distinct groups.

The bald eagle is a typical member of a group of about eight species known as sea eagles or fish eagles. Widespread in North America, Europe, Asia, Africa, Australia and many islands, they're most often seen along coastlines or around lakes and rivers. The golden eagle belongs to a group that includes about a dozen species, and they're also found on the same five continents. However, they generally live in dry interior country, not along coastlines, and they're less likely to be found on islands.

Although these two groups of eagles are equally widespread, the bald eagle itself is a specialty of North America, found only from Alaska and Canada south to northern Mexico. The golden eagle is widespread in North America, especially in the West, and it also lives across the wilder regions of Europe, Asia and parts of northern Africa.

FROM LEFT: MARIO CEA SANCHEZ/MINDEN PICTURES; D. ROBERT FRANZ/ROLFNUSSBAUMER.COM

Left: The wingspan of a golden eagle can reach 7 feet.
Above: An adult golden eagle feeds its young in a nest on a cliff.

On the Menu

Both of these eagles are powerful predators, and both species have varied diets. The tops of their menus are different, though: Bald eagles prefer fish, while golden eagles feed mainly on small mammals.

Bald eagles often hunt by flying over the water and then swooping down to grab a fish near the surface with their strong talons. They also steal fish that have been caught by other birds, like ospreys or other bald eagles, but they're just as likely to eat dead fish that have washed up on shore.

Golden eagles, by contrast, almost never eat fish. Their mainstays are mammals like jack rabbits, prairie dogs and ground squirrels, and they also catch large birds, such as grouse and ducks. And while this might not seem to fit with their majestic looks, both species are scavengers, taking advantage of easy sources of food like roadkill and other carrion.

A parent bald eagle feeds its young.

An adult bald eagle soars in flight.

A Nest Fit for an Eagle

Both bald and golden eagles build large nests out of sticks. In both species, pairs may use the same nest for years, continuing to bring new material to add to it each year, creating a massive structure. The two eagle species prefer different kinds of nest sites, however. Bald eagles usually place their nests in large trees, although they'll sometimes build the nest on a cliff or even on the ground on an island. Golden eagles usually choose a site on a cliff, but on flat land where no cliffs are available, they will build nests in large trees.

In both species, the female lays one to three eggs, with two being the typical number. And although each parent takes part in incubating the eggs, the female does more of it. The male often brings her food at the nest. After the eggs hatch, the female stays with them most of the time at first while the male hunts to bring back food for the family. Later, both parents will go off to find food for the growing eaglets.

Raising a family is a lengthy process for these big birds. Golden eagles incubate eggs for about six weeks until they hatch; then it's about another 10 weeks until the young learn to fly. For bald eagles, the incubation period is about five weeks, but it may be another 11 to 13 weeks before the young eagles take to the air.

No matter how many times you see an eagle, it always takes your breath away. The more you understand about their lifestyles and behaviors, the better you can protect their populations and ensure that future generations will also gasp in awe at the sight of these magnificent birds.

A MAJOR COMEBACK

Fifty years ago, bald eagles were seriously endangered. Their populations had been decimated by illegal shooting and especially by the effects of DDT and other pesticides. Fewer than 500 pairs were left in the Lower 48, and most of those pairs were failing to raise young. With increased protection, the eagles have made a spectacular recovery since the 1970s, and there are now well over 10,000 pairs in the Lower 48, plus many more in Canada and Alaska.

Swamp Things

When they're not lurking in wet, marshy places, spot these interesting creatures dancing in the sky.

A Wilson's snipe displays ruffled feathers as it wades through murky water.

TIMBERDOODLE. NIGHT PARTRIDGE. MUDBAT. LABRADOR TWISTER. MARSHDOODLE. BOGSUCKER. No, we aren't talking about imaginary creatures from a fantasy novel. Those are real nicknames for two of North America's most remarkable birds: the American woodcock and Wilson's snipe.

These two are alike in having round bodies, short legs, short necks, big heads and very long, straight beaks. Technically the woodcock and snipe are classified as members of the sandpiper family, but you won't find them on sandy beaches. Instead, they hide in marshes and swamps or deep in the woods. It takes serious effort to get to know them.

Secretive, Solitary Skulkers

Wilson's snipes lurk in marshes and wet meadows, sometimes venturing out along edges of muddy ponds. American woodcocks hide on the ground inside leafy forests and thickets by day, venturing out into overgrown fields at night. Even when they're out in the daylight, these birds are difficult to spot because they wear cryptic patterns of buff, brown and black. When they sit still, their camouflage blends in perfectly against a background of dry marsh grass or dead leaves on the forest floor.

Although usually not seen by most people, American woodcocks are common in southeastern Canada and the eastern states, mostly east of the Great Plains. Wilson's snipes are found from coast to coast across Alaska, Canada and the northern states in summer, migrating south to spend winter throughout the central and southern states and deep into Mexico.

The long, straight bills of snipes and woodcocks provide a clue to their feeding behavior. They locate food with their sense of touch: The tip of the bill is very sensitive, so when a bird plunges it into the mud, it can feel earthworms, grubs, snails and small creatures moving around. And the upper mandible of the bill is flexible, so these odd birds can open up their bills just at the tip to grab something deep underground. With eyes located high on their heads, they can watch for danger even when their bills are pointing down.

A woodcock's eyes are high on its head to keep a careful watch for predators while it forages.

When on the hunt, Wilson's snipes dip down, using their sensitive bills to catch worms, bug larvae, snails, crustaceans, and the occasional frog or fish.

Above: Identify woodcocks by their thin facial stripes, distinct shape and cinnamon underbelly.

Near right: A male American woodcock uses a unique call (and dance) to attract potential mates.

Far right: Woodcock chicks start their lives in an unrefined nest. It is placed on the exposed ground and features only a shallow bowl.

Flamboyant Fliers

At first glance, they don't look like skilled fliers. If you surprise a woodcock on the ground, it whirs off through the woods on short, rounded wings. The snipe leaps up from the mud and zigzags away as if it can't decide which way to go. Both species seem reluctant to fly most of the time. But on nights in early spring, they perform some of the most impressive sky dances of all North American birds.

The male woodcock starts his performance around dusk by standing on an open patch of ground and calling a loud, buzzy *pzeent!* several times per minute. Then he abruptly launches into the air and flies almost straight up, rising more than 100 feet above ground before he levels off. Then moving in a slow, fluttering circle against the darkening sky, he makes a thin, high-pitched twittering sound, punctuated with sharp chirps.

After a minute or two, he abruptly stops and dives toward the ground, landing exactly where he started, and begins making *pzeent* notes again. He may do this dozens of times during the first part of the night and again near dawn.

Wilson's snipes are faster fliers than woodcocks. The male may perform day or night, but even in daylight he can be difficult to spot as he zooms around the sky in huge circles. He's easy to hear, though, because every so often he goes into shallow dives while making a loud, hollow, quivering trill, often referred to as winnowing. The whole presentation isn't as fancy as the woodcock's artful display, but it may last longer, with the male snipe sometimes zipping around and winnowing for more than half an hour at a time.

As if the aerial displays of these birds weren't bizarre enough, they make sounds in flight not with their voices but with certain feathers. On the male woodcock, the three outermost feathers on each wing are very narrow, and they vibrate in flight to make a twittering sound. On the snipe, it's the outermost tail feathers that are shaped to vibrate, and the bird can control the airflow across those feathers by the way it beats its wings, creating the loud winnowing notes that echo across the marshes.

In their own ways, woodcocks and snipes dance in the sky to attract and woo mates and to assert their claims to a nesting territory. The flight displays and musical feathers are meant to impress others of their kind, but they also impress humans lucky enough to witness them.

The Ultimate Nomads

The unique bill of a male red crossbill and its relatives serves an important food-foraging purpose.

Random migrations are just one crossbill quirk—learn more fun oddities of these wandering species.

Traveling in large flocks, male and female red crossbills go where the cone crops are robust.

WALKING INTO A PINE GROVE, you hear soft, unfamiliar calls overhead. Looking up, you see a dozen small birds clambering about over the pine cones, acting like tiny parrots. Some are red, and some are dull yellow-green. Take a good look: These are crossbills, and they may stay put for a month or may be a hundred miles away tomorrow. Two species, red crossbill and white-winged crossbill, are widespread in North America. And they're among the most unusual birds in the world.

Unique Beaks

When you look at a crossbill's face, it's obvious how it got its name. The bill is thick at the base, but the mandibles cross over each other instead of meeting at their narrow tips. This shape would be awkward for picking up most items, but it's perfect for one thing—prying open the cones of pines, spruces, hemlocks and other evergreens.

For most small birds, getting seeds out of a cone is too complicated to be worth the effort. For crossbills, it's a snap. The bird inserts its bill between two cone scales and then closes it so that the crossed tips push the scales apart. Twisting its head, the bird works to reach the seed buried between the scales. Using its tongue against grooves on the inside of its bill, it pulls out the seed, cracks the dry husk and swallows the kernel. This happens in a lot less time than it takes to describe it—a crossbill can extract and eat more than 20 seeds per minute, which means better than one every three seconds!

Northern Nomads

When conifers are loaded with cones, these birds have an easy food source. But big cone crops don't last and are extremely variable from year to year, so crossbills move until they find the next good food supply. Crossbills might be abundant one year in a forest and completely absent the next.

In most kinds of birds, each male has a regular nesting territory and returns to it the same time every year to pair up and raise a brood of young. Crossbills throw those rules out the window. When a roving flock comes to a forest where lots of cones are ripening, they settle in, build nests and lay eggs. After the young birds are old enough to fly, if the seed supply is starting to run out, the flock may move on—and those particular birds might never visit that place again.

Crossbills don't follow the guidelines of a calendar or a map. They raise young at almost any time of year, whenever they find a good cone crop. For example, in one area of eastern Canada, white-winged crossbills have been found nesting at four different times in one year—in February, April, July and September—feeding on seeds of three different kinds of spruce.

Left: A white-winged crossbill uses its bill to easily pry open a spruce cone to access a seed. Above: A clear shot of a male red crossbill with its special bill.

Same Yet Different

Overall ranges of the two species overlap, but white-winged crossbills are mainly farther north, in spruce forests across Alaska, Canada and the northernmost states. Red crossbills occur from southern Alaska across Canada and the northern states, farther south in the Appalachians and in the western mountains, with other populations in the mountains of Mexico and Central America.

There's one unique thing about the red crossbill: It can be divided into 10 types in North America. These are not subspecies but groups separated by slightly different voices and by preference for certain trees. For example, Type 1, found mainly in the Appalachians, has a short, quick callnote and prefers the seeds of red spruce and eastern white pine. Type 2, widespread in the Rocky Mountains, has a deep, husky callnote and prefers the seeds of ponderosa pine. Type 3, most common in the Pacific Northwest but wandering widely, has a squeaky callnote and prefers the seeds of hemlocks. All of them wander widely across the continent, often overlapping but rarely interbreeding. Scientists are still trying to figure out if some of them should be classified as distinct species.

Wandering flocks of white-winged or red crossbills may show up far from evergreen forests, especially in winter. Occasionally they visit bird feeders for sunflower seeds, but you are much more likely to see them in groves of conifers, such as in parks or cemeteries. If you find a flock, count yourself lucky to meet the ultimate nomads of the bird world.

At left, a female red crossbill feeds its young brood in the nest, which can be as wide as 9 inches. At right, a male Cassia crossbill proves to be more colorful than its female Cassia crossbill counterpart, shown below.

THE ONE THAT STAYS HOME

Southern Idaho has its very own bird that is not found anywhere else in the world.

The Cassia crossbill looks very much like a red crossbill, and it wasn't officially recognized as a separate species until 2017. Although its relatives wander far and wide, the Cassia crossbill doesn't stray from the lodgepole pine forests of Idaho's South Hills and Albion Mountains. Why? Because the two areas have no red squirrels. In most places, lodgepole pine cones are quickly stripped of seeds by red squirrels, so the crossbills grab whatever seeds they can and then move on. But in these two isolated mountain ranges where there is no competition from squirrels, Cassia crossbills dine on those seeds all year without having to fly away in search of more.

Snow White

Embark on a winter adventure in search of these extra-special fliers named for their distinct plumage.

A snowy owl shows off its impressive wingspan.

Snow geese, shown here with a few Ross's geese at Bosque del Apache National Wildlife Refuge in New Mexico, migrate in flocks to their wintering grounds.

WINTER IS BUSY SEASON at the feeders, but to see most of these similarly named birds, you will have to go beyond the backyard. These species from different families have a wide range of habitats, from farm fields and grasslands to ocean beaches, each matching a specialized need.

Like human snowbirds, most of these birds move south for a winter stay in a warmer place. South can mean almost anywhere in the Lower 48, especially for the Arctic birds, so keep your eyes open for these snowy winter friends.

Snowy owl

Lemmings have been the butt of jokes since the myth of them committing mass suicide went mainstream thanks to faked scenes in a 1958 Disney movie. But lemmings are no laughing matter to a big white owl of the Arctic—the mouse-sized rodents are the snowy owl's main menu item. In winter, some snowies move south erratically, and individuals may show up as far south as Texas and Florida. They prefer grasslands but are also seen perched high on roofs or at landfills where they keep a lookout for rats—or to them, supersize lemmings.

Snow goose

A huge flock of snow geese rising from a farmer's field, swirling and honking, is an awesome sight. But these birds have become too much of a good thing, exploding in numbers over the past few decades. More than 5 million honk their way from Arctic tundra nesting grounds to winter quarters along the Atlantic and Gulf coasts and to inland fields and lakes. Voracious vegetarians, the vast flocks cause habitat-altering damage as they congregate and feed, affecting all sorts of other species. Snow geese often nest close to snowy owls in the Arctic. The owls' fierce defense of their own nests helps keep foxes and other predators away from goose nests, too.

Snow bunting

These spunky sparrowlike birds nest farther north than any other passerine, arriving in Arctic homelands when temperatures still dip as low as 20 below zero! In winter, they head south to open fields, shorelines and roadsides across all but the southernmost U.S. Look for these buntings in flocks foraging for weed seeds in fields or along shorelines. When the flock flies a short distance to a better spot, they flutter like windblown snow, which inspires their "snowflake" nickname.

Snowbird (junco)

Winter is coming! And the arrival of juncos is one of the first signs. Loyal feeder friends from late fall through spring in most regions, they are present year-round in the West and the Appalachians. Their gray hoods remind us of a stormy sky, with their white bellies being the snow beneath. Although they're called dark-eyed juncos officially, they have been known as snowbirds since before Audubon's day. Inexpensive millet is their favorite feeder seed.

FIRST SPREAD: JIM CUMMINS/SHUTTERSTOCK; PREVIOUS SPREAD: STEVE BYLAND;

Left: White feathers with rusty accents help snow buntings blend into a winter landscape.
Above: Although it doesn't officially have snow in its name, the dark-eyed junco is deemed the original snowbird.

Above: A snowy egret keeps close watch on the water, looking for its next meal.
Right: Sandy beaches are home to snowy plovers. The tiny birds blend right into the sand.

FROM LEFT: GAIL BUQUOI; RICHARD BUQUOI

Snowy egret

This small white heron is super easy to spot and ID—but only if its unique bright feet (on black legs) aren't under the water. Look for yellow toes most of the year or orange feet in the breeding season. Luckily, it frequently dashes after its aquatic prey, revealing those trademark tootsies. Find snowy egrets, often among other wading birds, on your own snowbird vacation to the Gulf or Atlantic coasts, where they live year-round, or during winter on the Pacific coast. The egrets nest in colonies—inland as well as on the coasts.

Snowy plover

The feast of billions of brine flies is quite the show at Utah's Great Salt Lake, one of the inland salt flats where snowy plovers breed. These shorebirds get their share of flies by running through the mass with open bills, snapping fast. Practically invisible when not in motion, the 6-inch birds are found year-round on the Pacific and Gulf coasts, or on inland salt flats during breeding season. Signs and seasonally restricted areas keep people from stepping on eggs or nestlings.

The Most Beautiful Birds

It's said that beauty is in the eye of the beholder, yet these nine species have universal appeal for their pleasing color palettes, their unique body lines and, sometimes, their hints of elusiveness. When it comes to these birds, you can't help but admire them.

◀ GREAT BLUE HERON

Spotting a great blue heron, a species that is widespread but never overly abundant, always feels like a treat. These regal birds fly with a majestic fluidity and look stately as they stand along the water's edge. With a lightning-fast strike, herons easily nab fish or frogs for a meal. Perhaps the one part of the great blue heron that's not as beautiful is its call. The rough squawk has a guttural, almost prehistoric sound to it.

▲ GREEN JAY

Green jays bring tropical flair to the Lower Rio Grande Valley at the southern tip of Texas. These vibrant fliers are enticed onto platform feeders. A bit cartoonish with greens, yellows, blues and black, the birds have black Groucho Marx eyebrows that give them extra character. If a trip to South Texas isn't in your immediate future, stream the feeder camera of the Sabal Palm Sanctuary to try to spot a green jay.

► PAINTED BUNTING

Another exotic-looking bird that occasionally visits feeders in the southern United States is the painted bunting. Males wear a rainbow of colors, while females are a vivid greenish yellow. Despite their brightness, buntings can be difficult to spot since they prefer dense thickets. Providing good cover habitat is as helpful as having bird feeders if you hope to host painted buntings in your yard.

PREVIOUS SPREAD: GAIL BUQUOI; THIS SPREAD, FROM LEFT: MARIE READ; STEVE AND DAVE MASLOWSKI

FROM LEFT: JOHN GILL; STEVE AND DAVE MASLOWSKI

◀ AMERICAN AVOCET

The American avocet's stiltlike legs and long, thin, slightly upturned bill give it a sense of gracefulness. The crisp black-and-white coloration of immature and nonbreeding adults is accented by rich, rusty peach hues along the head and neck of breeding birds. Mainly a species of the West, they nest along open bodies of water. While foraging, avocets swish their bills back and forth in the water in a technique known as scything.

▼ SCISSOR-TAILED FLYCATCHER

A long split tail gives Oklahoma's state bird a very distinct silhouette. Its salmon-colored shoulders and underwings stand out in flight. Like the closely related kingbirds, this species is often observed on open perches, ready to fly out to snag any insects in midflight. While the bird's core breeding range is in the south-central United States, individual scissor-tailed flycatchers have been known to show up in other locations around the country.

▲ BOHEMIAN WAXWING

Waxwings have a soft appearance, almost as if they just escaped from a watercolor painting. Bohemian waxwings roam south to eat fruits and berries in wintertime, sometimes commingling with flocks of cedar waxwings. The waxy red wingtips and yellow tips on their tail feathers are colored by carotenoids, which are pigments found in fruits the birds consume. Rusty undertail coverts and rich hues along the head help distinguish Bohemians from their more familiar cedar waxwing counterparts.

▶ WOOD DUCK

When it comes to ducks, this species is a strong candidate for the most dapper. The iridescent sheen of the crested head of the male is simply stunning. While the males are easy to spot for much of the year, they do molt into brown feathers for a short period in late summer. During this eclipse plumage, they are camouflaged when resting and closely resemble female wood ducks. Even while they are in this muted pattern, males maintain their bright red eyes and bills.

FROM LEFT: AGAMI PHOTO AGENCY/ALAMY STOCK PHOTO; RICHARD BUQUOI

FROM LEFT: LARRY DITTO; WILLIAM LEAMAN

◀ ELEGANT TROGON

Although trogons are a family of tropical birds found mostly south of the U.S. border, elegant trogons have a very limited range in the United States. They are worth seeking out in the wooded canyons of southern Arizona. Their distinct white chest bands offset their brilliant pink bellies and festive green heads. Long tails and portly bodies also help them stand out. Elegant trogons are secondary cavity nesters, meaning they take over and create homes in holes excavated by woodpeckers.

▼ SCARLET TANAGER

Simply stunning, tanagers are usually spotted in the forest canopies of the eastern United States. They can occasionally be coaxed into backyards with nectar, suet, mealworm or jelly feeders. Their fairly thick bills are used for eating insects and fruits. Male scarlet tanagers have dark wings and tails with bright red bodies, while females and immature birds are a greenish tone. The scarlet tanager's song is sometimes described as sounding like a sore-throated robin.

CHAPTER 4

Attract More Birds

Use the simple advice here to make your backyard a hot spot for years to come.

Spring into Action

When spring is in full swing, flowers are blooming, migrating birds are returning and days are warmer. This wonderful change of season calls for new strategies to make sure your feathered friends keep coming around.

Attract orioles, like this Bullock's, with oranges and jelly as they migrate through your area.

Left: A basic peanut feeder brings in songbirds of all kinds, such as this tufted titmouse and black-capped chickadee.

Below: Pygmy nuthatches, like this one, and other insect-eating songbirds stop by backyards that offer mealworms.

Feeders with small, shallow dishes are ideal for serving mealworms to eastern bluebirds.

Jelly attracts many species, including rose-breasted grosbeaks.

Just Keep Feeding

When springlike weather arrives, it's tempting to let feeders go empty. Remember that it's actually a critical time. Natural food is hard to find because wintering birds have eaten most of the weed seeds and wild berries, and as many hidden hibernating insects as they could find. So even as the temperature rises, local birds still need a hand, and your feeders may help get them through until more spring insects start to appear.

Suet up for Action

Suet—both raw beef suet from the butcher and commercially produced suet cakes—is a popular winter food. While it attracts birds in spring and summer, it requires more attention. Some kinds of suet cakes melt in warm weather, so look for those specifically designed as all-season bird food. And because raw suet turns rancid quickly in hot weather, it is wise not to use it after temperatures warm up in spring.

Mealworm Madness

Offering food other than seeds is an excellent way to attract new species to your yard. Jelly and mealworms are fine supplements to your standard offerings. Jelly is popular with many birds, especially orioles and catbirds, and mealworms tend to attract more insect eaters, like bluebirds. However, here's a word of caution about mealworms and jelly: It's best to serve them in moderation, offering only a small amount of these foods per day. If birds feed too heavily on these treats, they may run the risk of nutritional deficiencies.

Fruits of Their Labor

Spring is a good time to begin offering fresh fruit, such as orange halves, apple slices and grapes. These attract catbirds, orioles, robins and mockingbirds. Orioles are particularly drawn to oranges. It's possible to buy feeders to display these fruits, or just impale them on a pointed stick near your other bird feeders.

Suet provides birds like downy woodpeckers a high-fat meal.

A brush pile gives birds like the dark-eyed junco a safe place to hide.

Tidying up Is for the Birds

After a rough winter, a few fallen branches may be littering your lawn. Build a brush pile in a quiet corner of your yard instead of having the branches hauled away or burned. Brush piles are easy to create and provide much-needed shelter and cover for birds and wildlife.

Spring Cleaning

Mild days in early spring are ideal to assess the condition of feeders that have been out in the elements all winter. Check for cracks, broken perches or damaged baffles, and repair or replace them if necessary. It's an excellent time to give feeders a thorough cleaning. Clean up any seed debris around and under the feeders.

A northern flicker was drawn in by the bubbling, moving water in this bath.

A Moving Experience

Drip. Drip. Drip. This is the sound that will attract birds! In winter, it takes some effort to keep fresh water from freezing, but at least your local birds will know where to find the birdbath. As migrating birds pass through, the sound of moving water will lure them in. Adding even a simple dripper or bubbler will entice more birds, including colorful warblers and other insect eaters that don't usually visit feeders.

Hummingbird Guilt Trip

You're standing at a window when the first hummingbird of spring arrives, hovering in the exact location where the feeder was hanging last year, looking in as if to say, *Hey, where's my food?* To avoid the hummingbird guilt trip, we suggest having feeders filled and in place by early April in the southern states or by late April in the North. A saucer-style feeder is the easiest to clean, and the design discourages bees and wasps.

Keep a Calendar

Write down the first date you see or hear summer birds return or migrants passing through. It's a fantastic way to be more aware of the advancing season. Tracking when your wintering birds depart is more of a challenge. If you have regular winter residents—juncos, for example—make a note each day that you see them, starting in March. Eventually you'll know when you last spotted the birds before they started to head north. After a few years, you'll have a fun and valuable record of the timing of bird happenings in your garden.

Northern cardinal

“A bird a hundred feet away is merely a bird, but within arm’s reach it is an animated thing to marvel at.”

Roger Tory Peterson
BIRD-LORE MAGAZINE, 1935

GET STARTED

Begin with a tube feeder to welcome finches, chickadees, titmice and cardinals almost immediately. Those species seem to recognize the shape of the feeder, and their presence attracts other birds.

Blue jay

Best Seat in the House

Get closer views of feeding birds.

ONE VERY IMPORTANT consideration when it comes to setting up feeders is yourself! The better your view of the birds, the more you’ll get to enjoy them. So instead of putting feeders way out in the yard, set them up just outside a window, no farther than 15 feet.

Ultimately, the best seat in the house is wherever you can easily see the birds. “A feeder at the kitchen window can keep meal-times interesting,” says wildlife artist Heather Bartmann of Fort Collins, Colorado. Her main visitors are house sparrows, but even the most common birds are fun to watch if you can observe their behavior up close.

Remember to think of yourself first when taking care of your feeders. Make sure they are easy to access in all seasons, but especially in snowy weather when they will be busiest. Include larger feeders so you can go at least several days without refilling.

Try grouping your feeders on a multi-armed pole. That simple trick instantly cuts the cluttered effect of scattered feeders. It makes your assortment a single focal point, no matter what kinds of feeders you include, and ensures that you can see all of the action from your favorite window.

Nearly all backyard birds feel a bit uncomfortable out in the great wide open, where they’re visible to predators. The temptation of a feeder will overcome birds’ natural instinct to hide, but there’s no need to put birds in danger. And, besides, when they feel safe, they visit more often and linger longer.

For sheltering cover, enhance your bird restaurant with cosmos, sunflowers and coneflowers or with berry-producing shrubs. As a nice bonus, those plants offer additional food that you don’t have to buy!

Create a series of garden beds, shrubs or trees across the lawn so birds can hop, skip and jump from one to the next as they come and go from feeders.

Plant a small deciduous tree near the feeders for a landing zone. It’ll get a ton of use in all seasons as an inviting place to perch. And it may entice grab-and-go birds like jays, chickadees, titmice or nuthatches to stop there instead of flying out of sight to hammer at their seeds.

The final trick: Create a window shelf, a simple board nailed to the sill, “to enjoy the birds at very close quarters,” as ornithologist Roger Tory Peterson urged 85 years ago in *Bird-Lore* magazine. After all, the benefits of bird feeding are for you just as much as for the birds.

American goldfinches

GOOD CHOICES

People-foods like oranges, berries, apples and plums attract Baltimore orioles. Set out a feeder specifically for fruit or just stick an orange half on a sharp branch.

Off the Menu

Nine foods to avoid to keep your backyard birds healthy.

WHEN YOU SEE small, sweet creatures hopping along, it seems so harmless to draw them in with whatever snacks you have available.

Though the urge is fierce, try to resist. Dishes people consume are generally bad for birds in the same way that junk food is bad for us.

"Malnutrition is certainly a risk if birds aren't getting the food that they need," says John Rowden, senior director for bird-friendly communities at Audubon. "They can be undernourished, which makes them more susceptible to disease, so it could cause health or lethal consequences."

With that knowledge, here's a list of nine nibbles to avoid feeding your feathered friends.

1. BREAD

People often drop bread for birds. Because it causes them to become full quickly, fliers may skip foods with actual nutritional value.

2. RAW MEAT

It might seem like a good idea to set out raw meat as a winter treat, but it can go rancid and spoil—and attract unwanted guests. "As soon as you put raw meat out, it starts to transform because it's outside of a refrigerated environment," John says.

3. SEED AND NUTS SOLD AND MADE FOR PEOPLE

Sunflower seeds and legumes made for humans often have large amounts of salt. Birdseed is produced specifically for birds, leaving out the extra sodium.

4. BACON FAT

This fat is very salty, has additives and spoils easily. To make suet, get high-quality fat straight from the butcher, before it gets processed.

5. POTATO CHIPS

While this popular snack is often a staple at outdoor gatherings, it doesn't provide proper nutrition. Keep these tidbits for the people at your next picnic.

6. HONEY

You'd think birds could use the calories and sugar, but honey can grow mold in addition to becoming troublesome and sticky.

7. RED DYE

There's no need to add any food coloring to your hummingbird sugar water. The dye is harmful and won't attract more birds.

8. OLD BIRDSEED

Serve fresh seed to ensure your backyard friends aren't exposed to moldy or rancid food.

9. PET FOOD

Dog and cat kibble lacks nutrition for birds and may attract mice, rats or other backyard pests.

In the end, it all comes down to mind-set. "In their heart of hearts, people are trying to do the right thing, and what they want to do is help birds," John says. "Great; we want to encourage that, it's just finding the right foods."

GROW A BUFFET

Instead of shopping for birdseed, save time and money by growing native plants that produce fruit, seeds and nectar. Favorites include crabapple trees, sunflowers and salvia.

> "I don't feed the birds because they need me; I feed the birds because I need them."
>
> **Kathi Hutton**
> CINCINNATI, OHIO

WARM WEATHER TREAT

When temperatures reach 40 degrees or more, it's no longer safe to serve birds suet, lard and other fats that spoil. Instead, try this summer-safe option from Linda Popejoy of Concord, North Carolina.

Pseudo Suet

2 cups shelled, unsalted peanuts
½ cup raisins
2 to 3 tablespoons cornmeal

Blend peanuts in a food processor until they're the consistency of peanut butter. Then add the raisins and process to combine. Mix in the cornmeal and process again. Press into a mold of your choice and hang in a suet cage.

Bird-Approved Berries

Grow these plants to serve a mix of tasty treats.

Northern cardinal on winterberry

1 Winterberry

ILEX VERTICILLATA, ZONES 3 TO 9

A close relative of the Christmas favorite, holly, this hardy shrub tolerates almost anything nature throws at it. It grows best in moist, acidic soils and easily handles winter cold. To get berries, plant male and female types.

Why we love it: Unlike other holly, winterberry's leaves fall away during winter, exposing its red berries and creating a perfect setting for photos.

2 Cotoneaster

COTONEASTER SPP., ZONES 3 TO 7

A colorful plant throughout the year, cotoneasters produce pink, white or rose flowers in late spring. Leaves turn purple, red and bronze in fall when red berries develop, to remain in winter. Some cultivars can't take the heat, so research and choose a plant that thrives in your growing conditions.

Why we love it: Cultivars like Autumn Fire are more than just pretty—they're also pest-resistant.

3 Mountain ash

SORBUS SPP., ZONES 2 TO 7

Mountain ash is a fall beauty. Its leaves turn beautiful shades of yellow and red, and its berries red-orange. This small, low-maintenance tree reaches 10 to 25 feet tall and prefers acidic, sandy, moist soil.

Why we love it: These oval-shaped trees produce lovely white flowers in spring that are attractive to butterflies and bees, along with fruit-loving birds.

Black-capped chickadee on crabapple

4 Crabapple

MALUS SPP., ZONES 2 TO 9

Crabapple trees are as beautiful as they are hardy if you choose a cultivar with disease resistance. They tolerate a range of soils, growing best in full sun. Pink and white flowers bloom in spring, and the persistent fruit develops over the summer.

Why we love it: Available in varying shapes and sizes, there's sure to be one that fits your gardening needs.

Cedar waxwing on serviceberry

5 Firethorn

PYRACANTHA, ZONES 5 TO 10

Firethorn offers many benefits—just steer clear of its prickly thorns. The shrub can be trained to grow up a wall, sprouting white flowers in spring and orange berries in fall and winter. Research before planting to see if it's invasive in your area.

Why we love it: Food isn't all firethorns offer. In winter, birds use the branches as shelter, and come spring and summer, they build nests inside the glossy foliage.

6 Serviceberry

AMELANCHIER SPP., ZONES 2 TO 9

This tree's white spring flowers are followed by small, delicious berries that turn from red to purple as they ripen in the early summer. Serviceberry grows 10 to 25 feet tall when in full sun and in the lightly moist or damp soil it prefers. It also tolerates some shade.

Why we love it: If you enjoy cooking, serviceberry is the right choice—you just have to get to the fruit before the birds do! Try it in jellies, jams and pies.

7 Beautyberry

CALLICARPA SPP., ZONES 5 TO 11

Beautyberry typically grows 3 to 5 feet tall and equally wide. It offers splendid sights, developing pink and white flowers in spring and purple berries in fall. Some cultivars even have white or pink fruits. Full sun or light shade suits it best. It tolerates clay or sandy soils.

Why we love it: Beautyberry is a treat for more than 40 bird species. Native varieties are found across the southeastern U.S., and birds may scatter the seeds even farther.

Northern mockingbird on bittersweet

8 American bittersweet

CELASTRUS SCANDENS, ZONES 3 TO 8

Growing up to 30 feet, American bittersweet is a fantastic choice for adding year-round interest to your garden. Unlike other bittersweets, the American Revolution cultivar is self-fertile, so you need to plant only one to get fruit.
Why we love it: The berries not only tempt birds but are lovely in dried arrangements.

9 Coralberry

SYMPHORICARPOS X DOORENBOSII, ZONES 4 TO 7

Coralberry is an option for gardeners with a little space to fill. It sprouts lovely white flowers in the summer and round, coral berries in fall and winter. Coralberry has a mounded habit and grows between 2 to 5 feet tall and 4 to 8 feet wide.
Why we love it: This shrub is deer-resistant, has a suckering habit that helps with erosion on slopes and is a magnet for favorites such as cardinals and chickadees.

10 Black chokeberry

ARONIA MELANOCARPA, ZONES 3 TO 9

Black chokeberry requires little work, and since it reaches 3 to 6 feet tall and 6 feet wide, it looks wonderful as a single specimen or grouped with other plants.
Why we love it: Chokeberry grows black fruit that delights songbirds in fall. The fruit remains through winter, so you'll have plenty of visitors in the colder months, too.

9: COURTESY OF PROVEN WINNERS - PROVENWINNERS.COM; 10: ZOYA_AVENIROVNA/ISTOCK.COM

Welcome Winter Guests

Become host to a bevy of backyard visitors with these cold-weather tips.

House finch

ATTRACTING YOUR favorite feathered friends in winter requires a little extra effort. But it's worth it when colorful songbirds arrive, brightening up a snow-covered landscape.

GO NUTS!

Chickadees, nuthatches, brown creepers and woodpeckers all love to snack on peanut pieces. Mix the pieces with seed, or hang a special peanut feeder to attract extra attention. Peanuts in the shell are a favorite of blue jays. Watch for fussy jays to pick up several peanuts before choosing the perfect one.

CHOOSE PLANTS THAT PROVIDE HEARTY MEALS

The seeds and berries that linger in your winter garden attract hungry birds. Select plants with late-season and long-lasting fruit to provide a steady, nutritious diet for your winged visitors.

PROVIDE SHELTER

When all the leaves have dropped and most trees and shrubs are bare, it's hard for birds to find a safe habitat for roosting and shelter. It's easy to create a winter comfort zone by growing evergreen trees, bushes, vines and ground covers. Don't forget to leave up a few birdhouses.

American bittersweet vines provide berries and shelter for blue jays and other songbirds.

Shrubs give birds like tufted titmice a safe place to land as they wait for a turn at the feeders.

ADD WATER

A clean bird is a warm bird! Dirt-encrusted feathers don't insulate against the cold as effectively as clean ones do. Use an electric or solar heater to warm up your birdbath so birds can stay tidy and have a drink on icy days.

THINK AHEAD

The most ideal time to fill feeders and birdbaths is midafternoon, before the birds go to sleep, so they can eat well before settling in for the long, cold night. If temps dip below freezing overnight, add warm water to your birdbath in the morning.

KEEP TRACK OF VISITORS

By observing their comings and goings over the seasons, you'll know what birds to expect and when. You'll also learn about the habits of each of the visiting species. It's fun to write observations in a bird journal that you can look back at in years to come.

LEAVE A LITTLE GARDEN DEBRIS

Instead of doing a thorough cleanup in the fall, let the birds enjoy the seedpods, leaf piles, dropped fruit and other natural materials that you might usually clear away.

GET YOUR WHOLE NEIGHBORHOOD INVOLVED

Expand the habitat you are providing by inviting your nearby neighbors to participate. With additional space, perches and food available, you're sure to welcome more birds to your area.

CREATE AND MAINTAIN A FOUR-SEASON HABITAT

Once you attract winter birds, don't stop there. Make your yard a safe haven by providing food, shelter and water year-round.

Keep holly and other shrubs free of snow, so birds can make the most of them.

GENTLY CLEAR SNOW

Brush snow and ice off feeders and flowers, and keep berry shrubs clear. Birds are most vulnerable after a snow or ice storm, so make it easy for them to get to your offerings.

SERVE THEIR FAVORITE FOODS

A buffet of seeds, suet and fruit will delight winter birds. Also consider hanging different styles of feeders around your garden to boost the food supply.

BE SURE TO REMEMBER GROUND-FEEDING BIRDS

Sure, some seed is bound to fall from feeders, but take a moment to scatter birdseed on clear patches of ground, too, such as a sidewalk or patio. This way, birds like dark-eyed juncos will likely become regular visitors.

Sunflower seeds are the best choice for attracting a variety of birds.

CLOCKWISE FROM LEFT: STEVE AND DAVE MASLOWSKI; NANCY MACDONALD; WINDU/SHUTTERSTOCK

CHAPTER 5

Garden Know-How

Plan and grow a bounty of thriving plants with tried-and-true landscape solutions.

Create visual interest within a monochromatic flower bed by growing plants of varying heights.

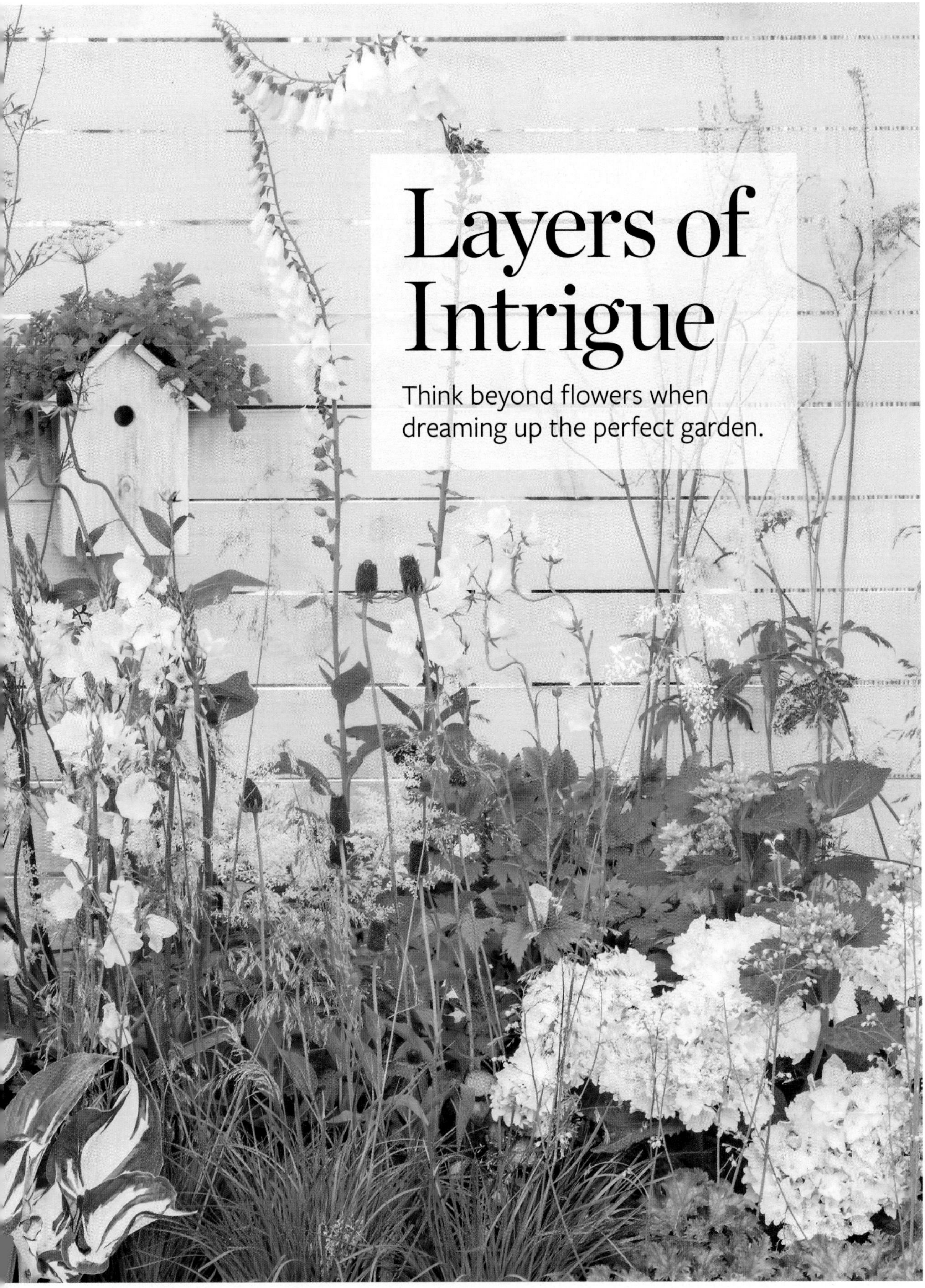

Layers of Intrigue

Think beyond flowers when dreaming up the perfect garden.

NO ONE CAN DENY the power of flowers. Whether in a bouquet or in a garden, they immediately command attention. It's primarily the color that catches the eye, whether isolated in a bold monochromatic statement or harmonized in a coordinated combo.

Just as there's more to a seven-course restaurant dinner than the rich dessert at the end, there's more to an impressive garden than colorful blooms. A number of other characteristics add layers of interest, including foliage, fragrance and form. Ideal garden design factors in many senses.

"It depends on what sense is most important to the people living with that garden," says landscape designer Dori Hein. "For some, fragrance or texture may be of more importance. For those favoring color, the question is, do they prefer a monochromatic scheme, a complementary scheme or a wild riot of color?"

Top: Towering archways covered in bright flowers establish a focal point. Bottom: Relax by a trickling fountain while enjoying floral scents.

Prioritize Your Senses

Dori, who has planned and planted a number of showpiece estate gardens in central Iowa, notes that plans should always be practical while also creating an inviting atmosphere. For example, structures, such as arbors and gazebos, give eyes some rest by hiding an unsightly view, providing privacy or offering shelter from wind or sun.

"Good garden design also factors in foliage and bloom colors and textures," she says. Foliage, in particular, is often overlooked. Evergreens are a must—not only do they provide year-round cover for birds but their shapes and sizes create a foil for flowers, especially for wispy species. In addition, deciduous plants lend season-long color with variegation or fleeting color with foliage that turns in the fall.

"Take into account how the landscape is used, whether it's mostly enjoyed through views from inside the house or from a patio or deck," Dori says. If you spend a lot

PREVIOUS SPREAD: GAP PHOTOS/ANNA OMIOTEK-TOTT • DESIGNED BY SARAH KEYSER, COUCOU DESIGN;

Ornamental grasses, like Northwind switch grass planted with heather and sedum, add eye-catching textures and height.

of time outdoors, you'll be more concerned with scent and sound than if you tend to appreciate the view from your living room window. In that case, form and movement would be a higher priority.

"Scent is especially welcome at entryways, where people often stop to congregate," she says. "Sound, such as soft chimes or a gurgling fountain, is ideal near seating areas and masks unwanted noise from street traffic." The rustling sound of trees is another example—the leaves move in the slightest breeze, providing a soft, soothing tone.

Create a Blueprint

Designing a garden from scratch may initially seem intimidating, but Dori has a few strategies. "Start at your front door and work outward, creating a pleasant and welcoming entry to your home," she says. "Don't be afraid to yank out overgrown shrubs and to prune trees to get more light."

When it comes to new homes with minimal existing landscaping, Dori suggests adding shrubs and other perennials that fill in quickly. Keep in mind that you will need to move some of those plants into new beds in a few years to avoid overcrowding.

Because flowers come and go, it's important to have good bones in the garden. That means structures, grasses and woody plants that have year-round presence. A bed of petunias is colorful but also flat. Add some rocks and creeping juniper to the front, and fill in the back with ornamental grasses and shrubs. This strategy adds height and texture for visual interest that won't disappear with the petunias when frost hits.

When planting, try to work in odd numbers. "Perennials look best when grouped in odd numbers—threes, fives and so on. Stagger the arrangement so it looks natural, though a highly contemporary garden can pull off rigidly perfect plantings."

In the end, it comes down to growing what makes you happy. "Don't be afraid to experiment with plants and to move them if they're in the wrong situation," Dori says. "Plant what you love, not what you think you should have."

Scent-Sational Flowers

Bring aromatherapy right to your home garden.

1: BRYTTA/ISTOCK.COM; 2, 3, 4: BALL HORTICULTURAL COMPANY

1 Sweet pea

LATHRYS ODORATUS, ANNUAL

Colorful sweet pea is sweetly fragrant when blooming in spring. It's also quite ornamental, thanks to the brightly hued pastel flowers of pink, purple and white. Give it something to ramble on and plant it where you can enjoy the scent—perhaps by a garden gate or near a frequently used doorway.

Why we love it: It's a cinch to grow and provides many fragrant cut flowers from spring until fall. It grows best in cooler temps.

2 Chamomile

CHAMAEMELUM SPP., ZONES 4 TO 9

If you're ready to relax, chamomile is the plant for you. Not only is the scent soothing, but so is the tea made from the plant. Roman chamomile (*Chamaemelum nobile*) is shorter than most ground cover, while German chamomile (*Matricaria recutita,* annual) is much more upright.

Why we love it: The white and yellow daisylike flowers appear in summer. Plant in a veggie garden to attract pollinators that eat pests.

3 Scented geranium

PELARGONIUM SPP., ANNUAL

Scented geraniums are enchanting plants to have around, even when they're not blooming, because the ornamental leaves have a wonderful fragrance. Scents include rose, pine, peppermint, apple-nutmeg and lemon. They're grown as are most geraniums, with plenty of sun and well-draining soil.

Why we love it: The leaves release their lovely scents when touched, so grow scented geraniums on a patio or in a window box for a quick whiff.

4 Rosemary

ROSMARINUS OFFICINALIS SPP., ANNUAL TO ZONE 8

Run the palm of your hand over the evergreenlike foliage and then inhale. You'll be in seventh heaven. Rosemary is a perennial shrub in Zones 8 and above and a tender annual herb in colder areas. Grow it in a pot and bring it indoors for winter if you have a bright southwest-facing window.

Why we love it: The oil's scent is said to enhance memory, and the herb is a powerful antioxidant.

5 Lemon verbena

ALOYSIA CITRODORA, ZONES 8 TO 10

Lemon verbena is easy to grow and an elegant addition to a landscape because of the leaves. They add a lemony flavor to teas and desserts and have an equally strong lemony fragrance when brushed. This is a perennial in frost-free areas. **Why we love it:** It's versatile. In southern climates, lemon verbena can grow into a 6-foot-tall shrub. In the North, grow it in a container and bring it indoors for winter.

6 Lily

LILIUM SPP., ZONES 3 TO 8

With elegantly shaped flowers in bright colors, some of them two-tone or offering intoxicating scents, it's easy to see why lilies are beloved among garden bloomers and cut flowers. Oriental types have an even sweeter scent. Lilies are simple to grow—if you can keep the rabbits and deer away. **Why we love it:** Lily plants bloom from spring to fall, depending on the species. Select several varieties for blooms all summer. They do best in sunny spots.

7 Lilac

SYRINGA SPP., ZONES 3 TO 7

As if the huge flower panicles weren't enough, Mother Nature also gifted the lilac enough glorious scent to put any perfume factory to shame. The soft fragrance is absolutely delightful and so are the flowers, which come in hues of lilac (naturally), purple, pink and white. **Why we love it:** One of spring's most anticipated sights and scents, lilac also draws in pollinators, and it serves as a fine nesting site for many songbirds.

5: WWASILISA/ISTOCK.COM; 6, 10: BALL HORTICULTURAL COMPANY; 7, 8: PHOTO COURTESY

8 Lavender

LAVANDULA SPP., ZONES 5 TO 10

Lavender is a colorful and fragrant garden herb. The flowers dry nicely and are often used in potpourri or bundled in sachets and kept in a sock drawer. Lavender is easy to grow if the site is sunny and has well-draining, slightly alkaline soil.

Why we love it: Bees and butterflies are drawn in by its lovely scent, while mosquitoes and flies avoid it. Snip a few blooms and enjoy the stress-reducing fragrance inside.

9 Mock orange

PHILADELPHUS SPP., ZONES 3 TO 11

Mock orange captivates in two ways: first with its yellow-centered white flowers and second with the blooms' sweet perfume. The scent is strongest in late spring, so be sure to get outside and enjoy it. It'll vary in size, from 18 inches to more than 10 feet tall, depending on the variety.

Why we love it: Its scented blooms attract a wide range of butterflies.

10 Sage

SALVIA OFFICINALIS, ZONES 4 TO 9

Common sage is a culinary staple, but gardeners who don't know their way around the kitchen like to keep it in the backyard for the soft, velvety gray-green leaves and delicate purple flower spikes.

Why we love it: Bees and butterflies—along with the occasional hummingbird—are attracted to the blooms, while deer ignore it.

Add interest to pots with creative combos, like sweet potato vine, lavender and tomato.

Blue Jangles hydrangeas are perfectly at home in containers.

The Perks of Pots

Use containers to jazz up entryways, hide garden eyesores, create privacy and more.

CONTAINER GARDENING is as hot as ever. People love pots because they're versatile—you can choose whatever styles, colors and sizes you wish—and they can be filled with an almost unlimited selection of plants.

While the very best-looking containers often feature one upright focal plant surrounded by sprawling fillers and falling spillers, anything goes.

"There's a general freedom to put in almost anything and everything—shrubs, annuals, perennials and bulbs, as well as decorative pieces," says Eric Liskey, owner of Landscapes by Liskey, a landscape design and installation firm in West Des Moines, Iowa. "It's a fun way to make a statement that reflects one's own style."

As a landscape designer, Eric sees the ways many gardeners use containers firsthand. He advises his customers not to be shy. "Go big! Large plants make a dramatic impact," he says. "Plants like cannas, ferns and elephant ears create a lot of 'visual mass,' which really makes a big statement."

Given a prominent position and massed for extra impact, containers serve many roles in the garden.

Pots of calibrachoa lend color and definition to the steps of an entryway.

HIDE AN EYESORE

Containers can mask an unsightly item or block a view. A group of stout containers can hide low-lying items like utilities and hose reels, while taller containers will cover even larger items. "You can use structures in containers, such as small panels, trellises and obelisks," Eric says, referring to the additional height they offer, "then grow vines on them to create a green screen."

DECORATE AN ENTRYWAY

Try naturally adorning doorways with containers, filling them with plants that reflect the landscape's formal or informal nature. Or take a few hints from your home's architecture. "Doorways often have strong vertical elements—trim, columns, windows—and I like to complement those with vertical potted plants," Eric says. "Grasses, cannas and bird of paradise plants are among the best."

ADD AMBIANCE

Real beauty is in the eye of the beholder—as is ambiance. "Plants definitely have a style," Eric says. "More contemporary homes and decor are complemented by succulents, spiky grasses, horsetails and sedges, while traditional homes tend to be enhanced by old-fashioned plantings such as fuchsias, begonias and trailers like bacopas. For a country feel, try daisy-type flowers such as black-eyed Susans, zinnias, coneflowers and asters."

PROVIDE A SENSE OF ENCLOSURE

If you have a patio or a deck, containers may be what you need to add privacy. "Don't overdo it," Eric says. "It does not need to be a solid wall. Just a few pots with the same, repeated design will mark the edge of the space and create the feel of an outdoor room."

MARK A GRADE CHANGE

"Containers make excellent visual markers that signal the transition from one space to another," Eric says. "For example, at the top of stairs, pots flanking the top step clearly define the transition."

While attractive plants are a bonus, they're secondary to the containers themselves. "Use large, heavy containers that are weatherproof so they can stay outside all year," Eric says. "Large urns can even be functional in this way without any plantings in them."

FEED THE POLLINATORS

One rather unorthodox use for containers is to attract wildlife, particularly the larvae of monarch butterflies. "Put a few medium to large containers in your flower beds and plant milkweed in them to attract monarchs," Eric says. "Some native milkweeds are aggressive spreaders, but in containers you don't have to worry about them."

Spikes of purple fountain grass add height and movement when grown with sedum and purslane.

7 TIPS FOR CONTAINER SUCCESS

Landscape designer Eric Liskey shares his best advice.

- Group containers in odd numbers—threes and fives—which feel more natural.
- Use multiple sizes for a more dynamic effect.
- Tie containers together visually with a shared material or color.
- Limit small pots to one species; large pots can accommodate three or more species.
- Create a stage for tall focal-point plants with mounding, monochromatic companions.
- Add extra color and texture with soil toppers such as marbles, colorful rocks or pine needles.
- Grow herbs and small veggies in pots if you don't have room for a vegetable garden.

Grow plants like Pink Hawaiian Coral peonies to discourage deer from eating their way through your garden.

12 Garden Allies

When dealing with challenges like heat, shade or space restrictions, picking the perfect plants makes all the difference.

HAVING A GARDEN often means sparring with forces of nature—including hungry deer, limited space and the baking sun. Proper plant selection is a gardener's most important tool in creating a beautiful backyard despite such formidable foes.

Start with a basic rule that would make any teacher or parent proud: Follow directions.

"Pay attention to the plant tag," says Donna Aufdenberg, a field specialist in horticulture for University of Missouri Extension. All the info you require—from size, to light, to watering needs—should be listed on the packaging. Match that information to where you plan on growing the plant to see if it's a suitable fit. She adds, "People forget to look up at power lines and phone lines—or don't give plants enough space. Pay attention to the hardiness zones." Using natives is another way to find plants that are low-maintenance and suited to your specific region.

To make your backyard a true knockout, turn to these 12 winning selections to overcome some of your peskiest garden challenges.

No, Deer

Yes, even foraging Bambis might turn up their noses at these plants.

1. BERGENIA

BERGENIA CRASSIFOLIA, ZONES 3 TO 8

Its nickname, pigsqueak, might be animal-inspired (its leaves squeak when rubbed), but most deer and rabbits say, "No, thank you." In spring, stems of pink flowers rise above large, glossy leaves. Often used as a shady ground cover, it thrives in dry soil and drought.

2. PEONY

PAEONIA LACTIFLORA, ZONES 3 TO 8

You'll eat up the showy, fragrant blooms of this classic beauty, but deer and rabbits won't. With tons of varieties and an array of flower forms and colors, peonies offer a lot to love. "It's an old-fashioned, fabulous flower that gives more than it takes," says Kathleen Gagan, owner of Peony's Envy nursery in Bernardsville, New Jersey.

3. WOOD SAGE

SALVIA X SYLVESTRIS, ZONES 4 TO 8

Sometimes called meadow sage, this perennial salvia has spikes of vibrant violet-blue flowers. Not only is it deer resistant, but it is also drought tolerant once established, is at home in the dry soils of rock gardens and hummingbirds love it.

They Like It Hot

Plants that say "no sweat" to hot, dry climates and drought.

4. BLUE MIST SPIREA

CARYOPTERIS X CLANDONENSIS, ZONES 5 TO 9

Sometimes called bluebeard, this deciduous shrub has rich deep blue flowers in late summer. In soil that drains well, it handles humidity and drought.

6

12

5. INDIAN HAWTHORN

RHAPHIOLEPIS INDICA, ZONES 8 TO 10

This compact and tidy shrub is a triple threat with fragrant pale pink or white flowers, glossy green leaves and wildlife-attracting berries.

6. COSMOS

COSMOS SULPHUREUS, ANNUAL

The Central American origins of this wispy yellow annual make it even better for toasty and dry conditions than the common pink and white *Cosmos bipinnatus*, and it is just as attractive to butterflies.

Shady Characters

Shine a light on these all-star plant picks that thrive in shade.

7. BUGLEWEED

AJUGA REPTANS, ZONES 3 TO 10

Its strange name leaves a little to be desired, but bugleweed is truly a showstopping perennial. It thrives in shade, acts as a ground cover, resists deer and has deep burgundy and purple leaves and spikes of pollen-rich purple flowers.

8. CORAL BELLS

HEUCHERA, ZONES 4 TO 11

There's a reason coral bells are a favorite for shady spots, and it is not the inconspicuous flower panicles. This perennial comes in a dizzying array of foliage colors, including purple, burgundy, red, orange, lime green and more.

9. PERIWINKLE

VINCA MINOR, ZONES 4 TO 8

The namesake periwinkle blue flowers of this evergreen creeper emerge in late spring. Thriving in shade and drought, periwinkle can overtake garden areas, so use it in spots where spreading is welcome and the plant isn't invasive.

Little Space, Big Impact

These plants pack a punch without taking up much room.

10. CORAL HONEYSUCKLE

LONICERA SEMPERVIRENS, ZONES 4 TO 9

The vines of coral honeysuckle grow up—not out—to infuse color into small spaces. The classic trumpet-shaped blooms attract hummingbirds, while fall berries feed birds. Plus, it isn't invasive like its nonnative relatives.

11. PROFUSION ZINNIAS

ZINNIA PROFUSION SERIES, ANNUAL

This series of zinnia varieties such as Profusion Red, Profusion White and Profusion Fire—you get the idea—packs vibrant color into small spots. Well-suited for containers, Profusion has won several All-America Selections gold medals. The plants are compact and disease resistant and bask in summer's hottest heat.

12. COLEUS

PLECTRANTHUS SCUTELLARIOIDES, ANNUAL

Who needs flowers when you have the bright, multihued foliage of coleus? The vibrant combinations of reds, greens and yellows and the wide variety of forms help light up partially shady spots and work well in containers or when planted in a small empty patch.

Decipher Plant Tags

Read the fine print to see if a top pick will thrive in your garden.

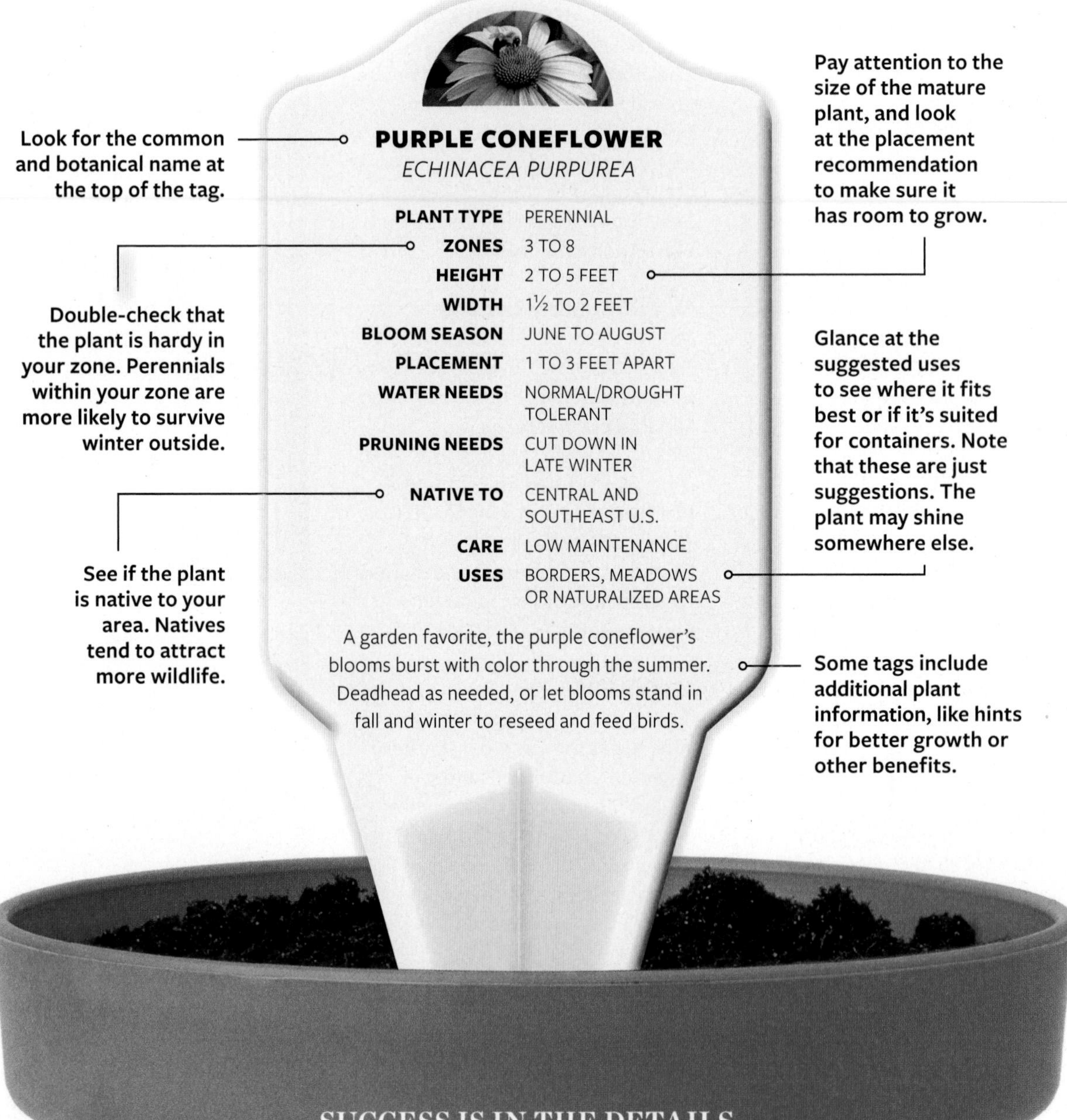

SUCCESS IS IN THE DETAILS

A plant may look beautiful at the garden center, but make sure it's right for your landscape before you hit the checkout line. Look at the light requirements, growing zone, bloom time and size. Every tag is a little different. If you have a question, use the botanical name to find more info online.

COCOA BEAN HULLS

A useful byproduct of the chocolate industry, cocoa bean hulls work in a variety of landscaping styles and don't compact over time. Use an inch-deep layer to help suppress weeds, but find another option if you have dogs—just like chocolate, the hulls are also toxic to them.

EVERGREEN NEEDLES

If you have conifers on your property, the fallen foliage makes excellent mulch. Rake out extra needles from under a tree and transfer a 1- to 2-inch layer to your beds. Contrary to popular belief, evergreen needles do not make soils more acidic.

WOOD CHIPS

Wood chips come in many forms, stay in place in windy conditions and can be very inexpensive. Ask your local municipality or utility company—it may give chips away for free. Pile on a 3-inch layer for weed-fighting benefits.

Master Mulch

Choose materials with the biggest benefits for your yard.

AUTUMN LEAVES

Recycle leaves for a quick way to put nutrients back into your beds. Shred with a lawnmower and use a 1- to 3-inch layer. Leaves may blow away with the wind, so consider taking the time to create a simple leaf compost for better results.

BARK CHUNKS

Look for medium and large chunks for the base of trees and shrubs. Bark is very attractive, comes in many colors and offers excellent weed resistance. Just keep the bark a few inches away from plant crowns and buildings to avoid ant and rodent damage.

ROCK AND GRAVEL

Fabulous for plants that need tons of drainage, rock or gravel is an attractive option that needs little maintenance. The downside: These materials don't improve the soil structure, add nutrients or regulate temperatures as organic mulches do.

Organic Pest Solutions

Use natural tricks to fight bad bugs and attract helpful fliers.

Watch praying mantises hunt bad bugs and, in turn, protect plants like this coneflower.

Encourage valuable pest-eating insects to stay in your yard with a bug hotel.

IT'S EASIER THAN you may think to manage pests while minimizing harm to pollinators, birds and the backyard wildlife you enjoy.

Start by picking plants that suit your growing conditions, indoors and out, and keep them in good shape to reduce the risk of unwanted attacks. When you first notice a potential problem, decide if control is needed. Only a small percentage of insects actually harm plants; the majority help you grow beautiful and productive gardens.

When harmful bugs bombard plants, consider waiting for predators and birds to step in and take control. Green lacewings, lady beetles, parasitic wasps and mantids like praying mantis are just a few of the insects that eat troublesome pests.

Outdoor Fixes

If you need to intervene, select the option that is most eco-friendly. Use a strong blast of water on outdoor plants to dislodge aphids and mites and to keep small populations under control. If you need to take pest control a step further, horticultural oils like Summit Year-Round Spray Oil and insecticidal soaps are superb organic choices. Bacteria- or plant-based insecticides like neem and spinosad are also safe alternatives for your backyard. Just be sure to read and follow label directions when using any chemical to avoid harming your plants or the environment.

Physical barriers are also effective. Shield your plants with floating row covers to prevent pests like cabbage worms, root maggots and Japanese beetles from dining on susceptible plants. Make sure to only cover those that don't require bees, butterflies or other insects for pollination.

Use traps to monitor and manage some pests, but avoid Japanese beetle traps—they will attract more of these unwanted visitors to your garden.

Healthier Houseplants

Always look for natural alternatives to keep you, your family and your pets safe when getting rid of pesky insects on indoor plants.

If you spot a pest, start your treatment with a quick shower. Wrap the pot in a garbage bag to avoid washing potting mix down the drain and give the plants a quick rinse. Follow with organic insecticides as needed.

For fighting whiteflies, enlist yellow sticky traps. They reduce populations to a level plants can tolerate. And, for fungus gnats, consider sprinkling bits of Mosquito Dunks on the soil surface and then water them in.

As you make the switch to organic pest control, you'll find an abundance of winged wildlife in your garden. And you can have peace of mind knowing your family and pets aren't exposed to harmful chemicals.

Plant a variety of flowers in your cutting garden for playful, eclectic bouquets.

Backyard Bouquets

Bring beautiful fresh-cut flowers indoors all season long from your very own cutting garden.

Collect blooms in the morning when flowers are perkier. Use a trendy wicker basket or, better yet, a bucket of water.

ONE LOOK AT THE PRICE of a bouquet and it's easy to see why cutting gardens have a loyal following. Growing a garden specifically for cut flowers is really a money-saver, not to mention that the bright beds look just like one of Monet's paintings—and that's before the flowers find their way into a charming bouquet!

"Having a cutting garden means bringing beautiful flowers and plants indoors whenever you choose," says Cynthia Haynes, associate professor of horticulture and extension specialist at Iowa State University. "Many of these flowers are not typically sold at local florists, so you will have something unusual as well." The variety of flowers you bring inside from your garden will change with the growing season, she adds, so there's little chance of getting bored.

Creative Selections

Cutting gardens predominantly feature annuals, which bloom longer and have a larger window of harvest than perennials. But remember, most bouquets are improved with a few sprigs of foliage—so other plants can play a role as well.

"I think annuals, perennials and woody plants all belong in the cutting garden," Cynthia says. "Peonies, irises, tulips and lilies are great flowers that every cutting garden should have."

She especially likes the year-round structure that woody plants and ornamental grasses lend to landscapes. Plus, they extend the harvest and provide seasonally changing material that adds interest to arrangements.

For example, forsythia's yellow spikes wow in early spring, lilac's fragrant blooms shine in late spring and red-twig dogwood's stems dazzle with holiday cheer in winter. And as for grasses, "ornamental plumes signal the end of summer and work well in arrangements after frost has killed many annual flowers," Cynthia says.

Pick the Perfect Spot

To start a cutting garden, you need little more than sun, soil and seeds. "Plants for cutting gardens are usually quite adaptable. As long as they receive full sun and have well-draining, fertile soil, most will thrive," Cynthia says. "Flowers for cutting gardens tend to be a bit taller than other annuals, so read the labels for mature heights and plan accordingly."

Some cutting gardens are picked often, so they should be placed in an out-of-the way spot where a drastic harvest won't be noticed. Others double as a display garden, meaning cuttings are spread out over time and don't seriously impact the look of the flower bed.

As for style and organization, Cynthia says cutting gardens are typically a jumble of colors. "A cottage-style approach works amazingly well in many landscapes. If you want a more tidy look, consider planting in designated spaces in orderly rows. This makes the flowers easy to harvest."

No need to worry if you have only a little space. "Sometimes I will plant a few annual flowers for cutting in open spaces between shrubs or where I have spring-blooming bulbs to occupy these spaces during the summer," Cynthia says.

Sow Early

Sow cool-season annuals such as larkspur, bachelor's buttons, poppies and calendula in early spring, but wait until the danger of frost has passed before sowing heat-loving zinnias and sunflowers or planting summer bulbs such as gladiolus and dahlia. Other annual flowers such as celosia, floss flower, lavender, lisianthus, snapdragon and statice also can be grown from seed, but they should be started indoors and then transplanted outdoors later.

"Start them yourself or buy transplants from a local garden center in spring. Both options are relatively inexpensive and typically grow well," Cynthia says.

Gather the Bounty

Cut flowers in the morning when it's cooler and blooms are fresher. Look for blossoms that are in bud, showing a bit of color, or just before peak bloom. Bring a vase or bucket out to the garden and place stems in water immediately. "The less time they go without water, the longer they will last," Cynthia says. "Besides a floral solution (little packets from a florist), don't add anything to the water."

Create an arrangement and place it where it's easily admired, such as on a mantel, dresser or coffee table or in a well-trafficked entryway, and enjoy the sights and scents of the garden throughout the growing season.

Dahlias

BOUQUET FAVORITES

ANNUALS	PERENNIALS	WOODY PLANTS
African marigold	Coneflower	Fothergilla
Cleome	Daffodil	Hydrangea
Cosmos	Daisy	Pussy willow
Gaillardia	Delphinium	Rose
Gloriosa daisy	Liatris	Yellow-twig dogwood
Phlox	Rudbeckia	
Salvia	Yarrow	

PREVIOUS SPREAD: GAP PHOTOS/ROBERT MABIC; THIS SPREAD, FROM LEFT: GAP PHOTOS; GAP PHOTOS/JULIETTE WADE

Showstopping Tulips

Plant these spectacular bulbs in fall for outdoor color and indoor vases.

This greigii is one of just 15 types of tulips. Each group has its own unique features and forms.

1 Mary Ann

TYPE: GREIGII; **BLOOM TIME:** EARLY SPRING

Low-growing greigii tulips are native to Central Asia. Their striped, wavy leaves are as big an attraction as their cup-shaped flowers, which splay wide open in sun and then close up at night. Some gardeners find greigii to be more long-lived compared to other tulip types.

Why we love it: Mary Ann is a head turner, with magenta and white petals that mature to pale pink and raspberry. Blue-gray-green leaves are delicately striped with burgundy.

2 Midnight Magic

TYPE: DOUBLE (PEONY FLOWERED); **BLOOM TIME:** LATE SPRING

Double early tulips light up any spring landscape with fresh color but are subject to whims of rain and wind. Double late tulips extend the growing season with longer-lasting bloom power. Double tulips, both early and late, often resemble peonies.

Why we love it: Midnight Magic, a double late type, offers fragrance from its deeply saturated red to burgundy petals. It works well with yellow, white or orange tulips in the garden or a vase.

3 New Design

TYPE: TRIUMPH; **BLOOM TIME:** MIDSPRING

Triumph tulips bridge the bloom season between single early tulips and Darwins. Best considered as annuals, triumphs are the largest category of tulips, blooming in a wide variety of colors.

Why we love it: Silky pink petals are enhanced with a creamy base on the outside and darker pink on the inside. But the leaves, rimmed with ivory to palest pink, really set New Design apart.

4 Estella Rijnveld

TYPE: PARROT; **BLOOM TIME:** LATE SPRING

Parrot tulips, as their name implies, are puckered, fringed, scalloped and feathered—a bit like the plumes of the flamboyant bird.

Why we love it: Estella Rijnveld may be an heirloom but it is still exciting. The flurry of red-and-white petals wave in the breeze like a cheerleader's pompom on a stem. Plus, it's a stunner as a cut flower.

5 Yume no Murasaki

TYPE: LILY FLOWERED; **BLOOM TIME:** MID-TO-LATE SPRING

Lily-flowered tulips grow with sharply pointed petals similar to the style favored in the Ottoman Empire, adding an elegant touch. Even when closed, the vase-shaped buds look exotic.

Why we love it: The rich purple flair of Yume no Murasaki opens to show a white base, especially on sunny days.

6 Artist

TYPE: VIRIDIFLORA; **BLOOM TIME:** LATE SPRING

Viridifloras—from the Latin words for *green* and *flower*—boast vivid green stripes along the centers of their petals and rank among the longest-lasting tulips, blooming up to three weeks.

Why we love it: The unusual coloration of Artist, one of the first viridiflora tulips, shows ingenious elegance during the life of the bloom, transforming from bright orange with green and purple markings to peach, olive and lavender.

7 Exotic Emperor

TYPE: FOSTERIANA;
BLOOM TIME: EARLY SPRING

Fosterianas, also called emperor tulips, are descendants of wild tulips from Central Asia. Some of that tenacity remains in these early-spring favorites that reliably return year after year.

Why we love it: Exotic Emperor, with its elegant semi-double creamy blooms, becomes paler over time, enhanced by yellow and green on its exterior petals. It does well in pots.

5, 9, 10: COLORBLENDS.COM; 6, 7: LONGFIELD-GARDENS.COM; 8: PHOTO BY 'BRENT AND BECKY'S'

8 La Belle Epoque

TYPE: DOUBLE (PEONY FLOWERED); **BLOOM TIME:** LATE SPRING

Double tulips—both early and late—present extra flower power. The blooms grow up to 4 inches across, and many offer interesting scents.

Why we love it: La Belle Epoque presents a fresh color palette. Dusky rose, peach, caramel and butterscotch tones ripple quietly throughout this beauty, which pales over time.

9 Banja Luka

TYPE: DARWIN HYBRID; **BLOOM TIME:** MIDSPRING

Darwin hybrid tulips are big, bold and brassy. Introduced in the U.S. in the 1950s, they are a cross between single late tulips and early fosteriana tulips, with large, sturdy flowers that rebloom several years after their first big burst.

Why we love it: Banja Lukas shine with gold petals streaked with orange-crimson. Plant them with solid purple tulips to pair in a vase.

10 Lilac Wonder

TYPE: SPECIES; **BLOOM TIME:** MIDSPRING

Species tulips form a huge group of wild types from which all modern tulips were developed. The small, tough plants are ideal for rock gardens or places with excellent drainage.

Why we love it: With unusual rosy lilac petals and a deep yellow center that glows like a searchlight, Lilac Wonder is a true charmer, reaching only 6 to 7 inches tall.

Divide and Multiply

Why splitting perennials is healthy for your plants—and even better for your backyard.

A gardener splits rudbeckia with shovels to create two smaller plants.

FROM LEFT: GAP PHOTOS/JONATHAN BUCKLEY - DEMONSTRATED BY CAROL KLEIN; MALIVAN_JULIIA/SHUTTERSTOCK

ONLY IN GARDENING does division turn into multiplication. We're talking about the process of dividing plants—digging up clumps of crowded perennials and splitting them into smaller individual plants.

"Dividing perennials gives you more plants to place in your landscape or to share," says Justin Hancock, horticultural craftsman for Monrovia Nurseries. And, of course, there are more perks to dividing plants. Just be sure they are pest- and patent-free first.

"The biggest value in dividing perennials is that it keeps most plants healthy and looking their best," Justin says.

While not all perennials and grasses need to be divided, the process can help reinvigorate them and encourage them to produce more blooms. It's usually plain to see when they are ready for a breakup.

"The most obvious sign that your plant could use dividing is when you see it start to die in the middle—as it grows, it is literally crowding itself out," Justin explains. "Other signs may be a decrease in flowering and overall performance. And the clump may be quite large."

Some plants can be split at almost any time, such as daylilies, but the best season to divide spring or summer blooming perennials is in fall, at least a month before the ground freezes. Wait until spring arrives to divide plants that bloom in fall.

Perennials with finer roots are among the easiest to divide. Plants like yarrow, monarda, coreopsis, and aster are simple enough to split with a spade. Ornamental grasses are more tricky. "The bigger or deeper the root system, the more challenging the physical dividing can be," Justin says.

To lessen the stress on the plant, Justin recommends digging holes for the daughter divisions before digging up the mother plant. "That can greatly reduce the amount of time your plant is out of the soil with its roots exposed," he says.

Justin also advises trimming plants to compensate for lost roots. "Roots absorb moisture for the plants, and leaves release moisture as they breathe," he says. Cut back foliage to reduce burden for roots and to help new plants establish.

Hosta

SPLITTING HOW-TO

Take these simple steps, and you will be dividing plants in no time.

GET STARTED

1. Dig up the plant you're splitting with a spade or fork on a cool, cloudy day.
2. Lift the plant to remove any loose soil and to tease the roots apart.
3. Separate the plant into smaller divisions, making sure each piece has growing shoots and roots.
4. Replant immediately and water thoroughly.

SIZING UP PLANTS

- Pull small plants apart by hand.
- Slice medium-sized plants with a sharp spade or serrated knife.
- Split large root clumps with two spades.

THE MORE, THE MERRIER

Perennials especially easy to split:

- Ajuga
- Aster
- Astilbe
- Chrysanthemum
- Daylily
- Goldenrod
- Hosta
- Leucanthemum
- Rudbeckia
- Siberian Iris
- Yarrow

Grow a Memory

Pay tribute to a special person or occasion by planting something meaningful.

Luke planted a hickory tree (above) in memory of his three uncles who fought in World War II. Each spring these beautiful buds emerge (left).

HICKORY BUD: BERNARD LYNCH/GETTY IMAGES; SILVER MAPLE: CRYSTALTMC/GETTY IMAGES

Luke's dad planted a silver maple tree to mark his birth.

LAST FALL I MADE a detour on my way to the airport. Wrapping up a visit to my hometown, I wanted to see one last friend before getting on the plane. I live a thousand miles away now, so it's not often that I get to see the tree my dad planted for me when I was born. It may be just a silver maple to some, but it's my silver maple.

Through the years I've continued this tradition. When my nephew Nick was born, I planted a black walnut to mark the occasion. I paid $2.50 for the seedling, but it was priceless to hear Nick had made a pilgrimage to see the tree decades later. I had always made it plain to him that it was his tree, and he felt a sense of ownership.

Recently I planted another black walnut—for a different reason. This one was growing sideways through the seam of a raised bed, and that tenacity inspired me to rescue the seedling. I dedicated it to a friend who has faced many obstacles since emigrating from Russia. I send him pictures of the tree's progress to remind him that he shares the same strength.

Choose any plant when marking a special occasion or person; just research the pros and cons of the plant first. Trees are my go-to simply because of their longevity. It is as close as we can come to earthly immortality.

A few years ago I found a maple seedling growing at my mom's gravesite. I dug it up, nurtured it in a pot until it put on some size, and then planted it in my yard. It has now been joined by three hickories—one for each of her three brothers, all World War II veterans with hickorylike fortitude.

As for my dad, the person most responsible for my love of trees, this year I'm sprouting an acorn I found under his red oak tree at the old family homestead. I also have a cigar tree that I rescued from Notre Dame, his alma mater. Although the tree lingered in a container for years before finding a permanent home, it's now quite content—and so am I whenever I look at it and take a sentimental journey home.

-Luke Miller

MAKE IT PERSONAL

Pick the right plant for the occasion.

- Plant a tree to mark a birth. Photograph the child with the tree annually to compare the growth—and to reinforce his or her bond with the tree.
- Select a decorative shrub to commemorate a big event, such as an anniversary or wedding. Choose one that blooms at a fitting time.
- Celebrate a special pet with a perennial. It will bring fond memories every year when it reemerges from dormancy.
- Choose a self-seeding annual for a departed loved one. You can collect seeds and share them with others who were close to the person.
- Grow a species to remind you of an ancestral home, whether it's English lavender, Mexican sunflower, Japanese painted fern or African daisy.

Midnight Hues

Dark petals add mystery and a fresh alternative to pastels and bright colors.

1: BALL HORTICULTURAL COMPANY; 2: EVA LECHNER/GETTY IMAGES; 3: VISIONS BV

1 Dark and Handsome hellebore

HELLEBORUS 'DARK AND HANDSOME', ZONES 4 TO 9

Part of the Wedding Party series, Dark and Handsome steals your heart with black-purple good looks. Hellebores thrive in part to full shade. After the blooms fade, attractive leathery green foliage remains.

Why we love it: This sturdy chap stands its ground when facing ravaging deer and rabbits and quickly naturalizes in woodland gardens.

2 Chocolate cosmos

COSMOS ATROSANGUINEUS, ZONES 9 TO 11 OR ANNUAL

Chocolate cosmos sprout from tender tubers that can be grown as annuals or brought inside for winter in cold climates. They ultimately reach up to 30 inches tall, growing best in a sunny garden patch. They shine from midsummer into fall and are easy to care for.

Why we love it: This cosmos is an absolutely luscious, calorie-free form of chocolate. The smell of the blooms even brings to mind red velvet cake.

3 Black Barlow columbine

AQUILEGIA VULGARIS 'BLACK BARLOW', ZONES 3 TO 9

This deep maroon, almost black double-petaled columbine adds drama to a late spring garden. Grow this 24- to 30-inch perennial in sun or part shade. It's short-lived, but it self-sows like a champ.

Why we love it: It sounds as if it was named after a pirate, and it may rebloom if it's deadheaded.

4 Black Knight hollyhock

ALCEA ROSEA 'BLACK KNIGHT', ZONES 4 TO 9

Black Knight scores with deep purple-black blooms even in its first year. If planted in full sun, this 5- to 6-foot-tall butterfly and hummingbird magnet will readily self-sow.

Why we love it: It is truly a perennial, not a biennial like most hollyhocks. It also grows within range of troublesome black walnut tree roots and resists rust.

5 Halloween Improved pansy

VIOLA X WITTROCKIANA 'HALLOWEEN IMPROVED', ZONES 6 TO 8

This black pansy is all treat, no trick—a step up from a pansy named Halloween II. Halloween Improved has fewer white stripes and more blooms than its predecessor. Plant this cool-season favorite in spring or fall.

Why we love it: It's spookily pretty and very festive when paired with orange pansies.

6 Queen of Night tulip

TULIPA 'QUEEN OF NIGHT', ZONES 3 TO 8

Glistening deep maroon petals masquerade as black. Pair this queen with bright and cheery orange or pink tulips placed in well-draining soil in a sunny spot. Plant in fall for spring flowers.

Why we love it: A favorite since the 1940s, Queen of Night is as mysterious as tulips get. If you want more petals, check out Black Hero.

7 Crazytunia Black Mamba

PETUNIA HYBRID 'CRAZYTUNIA BLACK MAMBA', ZONES 9 TO 11 OR ANNUAL

Velvety and dark, these are considered the best almost-black petunias you can grow. Plant these branching petunias in full sun for the best bloom power. Hummingbirds love them, even without bright color.

Why we love it: No deadheading needed! The old flowers drop off as they start to wilt.

5: BALL HORTICULTURAL COMPANY; 6: JOHN RICHMOND/ALAMY STOCK PHOTO; 7: DEBORAH VERNON/ALAMY STOCK PHOTO

8 Black iris

IRIS CHRYSOGRAPHES, ZONES 4 TO 8

It's hard to find a true black flower, but this iris is very close. Grow it in sun to part shade among perennials with rounded leaves so its spiky plumes peek out of the mounds. Irises attract butterflies and hummingbirds, and they make lovely, velvety dark cut flowers.

Why we love it: Blooms are elegantly held aloft slender 18- to 20-inch green stalks.

9 Persian lily

FRITILLARIA PERSICA, ZONES 4 TO 8

Persian lilies provide architectural intensity to a spring garden, with 20 to 30 dark plum, bell-shaped blooms lining up in alternating rows on slender stalks.

Why we love it: Though around since 1573, this perennial is still not widely planted. The blue-gray deer-resistant foliage alone makes it worth a shot.

10 Black Satin dahlia

DAHLIA 'BLACK SATIN', ZONES 8 TO 11

Growing 4 to 6 feet tall, this formal decorative dahlia produces large pompon flowers. The chocolaty poufs are edged with a deep burgundy flare.

Why we love it: One of the biggest perks is that the more flowers you cut, the more flowers you will get. Snip the long stems to pair with brightly colored blooms, creating an uplifting accent.

Make a wreath of birch bark and pine cones. Add a cup of suet for birds.

FROM LEFT: GAP PHOTOS/ELKE BORKOWSKI; BACK TO THE ROOTS; PULLIA/SHUTTERSTOCK

Until the Ground Thaws

Nine fun ways to fuel your love of gardening, even in winter.

THE YARD MIGHT be snow-covered and the air a bit chilly in winter, but you can still use your green thumb. For nature lovers, January, February and early March often spark impatience, but fret not—we've got you covered with gardening activities to pass the time.

1 Find Treasures

Even if it's covered in snow, your yard provides a great pastime: wreath-making. Head outside and grab red dogwood and a few birch branches—and some berries from the garden or a craft store—to construct a nifty, one-of-a-kind decoration that makes a delightful conversation piece or holiday present. To make the final product even more eye-catching, add a few dried flowers from last summer's garden.

2 Try a Mushroom Kit

A mushroom kit, like the one below from Back to the Roots (*backtotheroots.com*), offers an enjoyable, uncomplicated way to grow food in winter. These kits typically include a box or a log already seeded with spores. Keep the kit moist and at a constant temperature to see results with edible varieties, such as shiitake and black oyster. Mushroom kits are low-maintenance and don't require the same weeding or watering a garden does, but with so many types available, you might find your family's new favorite ingredient.

3 Be Scrappy

Wait, don't throw out that carrot top! Many veggies and herbs—carrots, celery, ginger, potatoes, peppers, basil, radishes and more—are comeback champs, as long as you keep the right part of the plant (usually either the top or the seeds inside) to stick back in the soil. If you feel the need to do a little research on the subject before plunking that radish top into the dirt, you'll find plenty of books and online materials on the subject. And best of all, it's a zero-risk activity: There's nothing to lose if no sprouts form, but you'll have much to gain if they do.

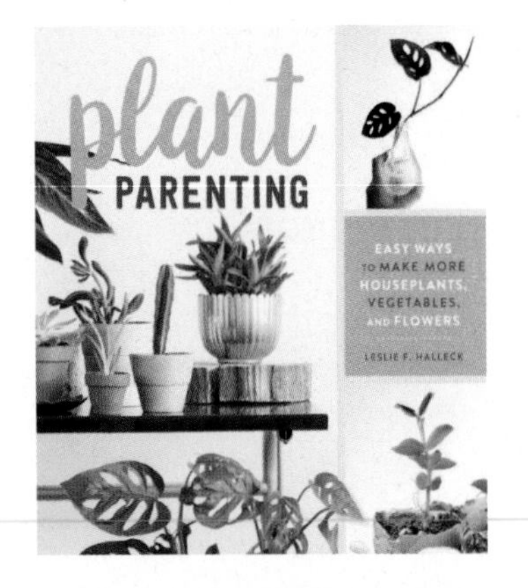

4 Become a Bookworm

With plenty of wonderful titles available, there's no time quite like winter to curl up with a blanket and a good book—and no matter your level of gardening experience, there's always something new to discover. *Buffalo-Style Gardens* by Sally Cunningham and Jim Charlier, *Edible Paradise* by Vera Greutink and *Plant Parenting* by Leslie F. Halleck (above) are a few fabulous titles to sit down with.

5 Dream Big

It is never too early to start planning for that wonderful spring thaw, so take the opportunity to write down your plans for the warmer seasons. Draw a diagram of where certain plants could go, research new ideas and circle your must-haves in catalogs. As long as the ground isn't covered, go outside and take measurements of your garden, too, to make sure you're using every inch available.

6 Get Crafty

If your pots are in need of some upkeep, it's the perfect time to tidy them up or even make them dazzling. Remodel your plants' spring and summer homes with paint or mosaic tiles, convert their bases to chalkboards with special types of paint, artfully cover them in newspaper or coordinate their decoration to match the plants you're planning to place in them. Newly bedazzled pots make great gifts! This applies to tools, too; you can decorate their handles with paint or glitter.

Use paint to add a little flair to concrete, wood or terra-cotta pots.

BOTTOM LEFT: STUDIO LIGHT AND SHADE/SHUTTERSTOCK; RIGHT: AFRICA STUDIO/SHUTTERSTOCK

Nurture succulents or houseplants to keep your green thumb going.

7 Do a Checkup

Winter is a perfect time to evaluate your houseplants and give them the care they might have lacked during the summer months. Determine whether they are getting enough water and sunlight, make sure they are bug-free and healthy, and divide or repot them in late winter. Fertilize houseplants that are still growing in spring. If you're yearning for another indoor plant pal, the chilly winter months could be a good time to rescue one from store shelves.

8 Get a Head Start

Some plants need to be started in winter to grow in summer. If you're yearning to plant something that'll stay with you through the next few seasons, get going on next year's crop. Veggies like spinach, kale or cabbage can be started indoors during winter. For maximum ease, use biodegradable pots that can be planted directly into the spring soil with your chosen vegetables.

9 Make Your Own Terrarium

- Place small pebbles at the bottom of a clear glass container for drainage. Add a layer of activated charcoal, which will absorb odors and keep the terrarium fresh.
- Add potting soil. If you want to grow succulents or cacti, mix the soil with sand using a funnel. Create layers of potting soil, sand, colored pebbles, etc.
- Choose a selection of small, slow-growing plants and plant them. Let your imagination help create a miniature world. Cacti and succulents are ideal for uncovered terrariums. Or use ferns, baby's tears, variegated spider fern, nerve plant or black mondo grass in a covered terrarium.
- Make the planting your own by adding seashells, colored beach glass or figurines.
- Place terrarium in indirect sunlight. Too much light can burn plants.
- An uncovered terrarium needs very little water. Check the soil, and water it just enough to moisten the potting mix.

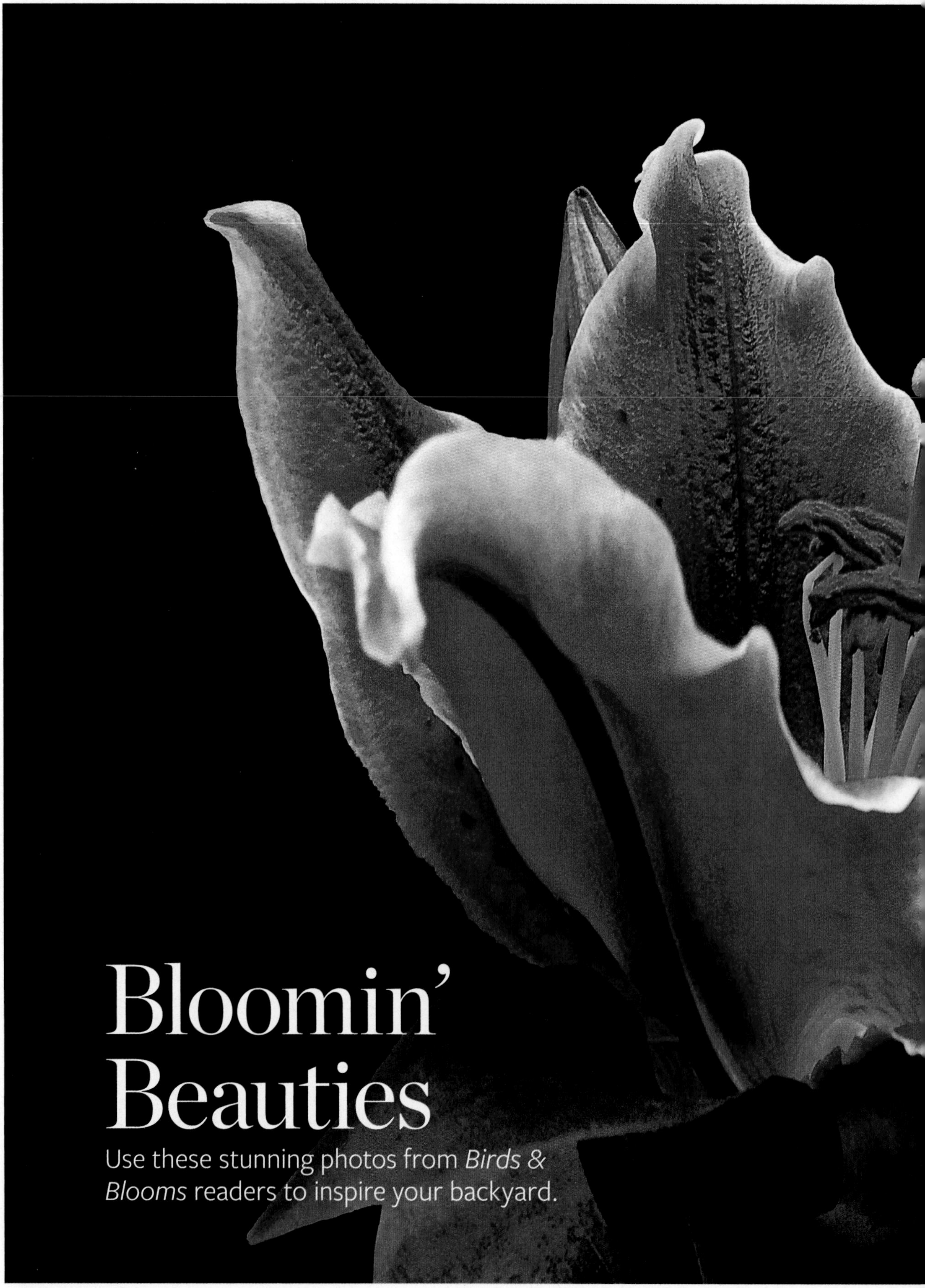

Bloomin' Beauties

Use these stunning photos from *Birds & Blooms* readers to inspire your backyard.

I love to take close-ups of flowers because the delicate inner beauty is one of the best parts of the plant. This was the largest lily I'd ever seen. The color, as well as the fine texture of the petals, had to be captured and shared. It has always been mesmerizing to me.

Diane Hendler
CORNVILLE, ARIZONA

▲ **A visit to** Gibbs Gardens in north Georgia is a lovely experience because the ponds have so many beautiful waterlilies. I like to get level with the water and capture the reflections.

Sara Aspy
MARIETTA, GEORGIA

► **I planted a pot** of zinnias with hopes of attracting hummingbirds and butterflies. I didn't ultimately get the activity I was looking for, but I was thrilled with how beautiful the flowers turned out. They were definitely the most gorgeous flowers in my backyard that year.

Donna Ruiz
CAMERON PARK, CALIFORNIA

◄ **Yellow roses** were my mother's favorite flower. I believe different species of plants have distinct personalities, and the rose—with its delicate petals—stands above all the others.

Lisbeth Rutt
ST. AUGUSTINE, FLORIDA

▼ **This sweet** bay magnolia blossom opened up just after a rain. I think these magnolias are lovely, and the center of the bloom is so intricate. Because this was only the second bloom I've had on this small tree since planting it, I was excited to capture this photo.

Gabrielle Harrison
FLORAL CITY, FLORIDA

Morning glory vines take over my deck every summer. I appreciate them in all their simple beauty as the sun shines brightly on the blooms and bees buzz around.

Lori Hayden
LOUISVILLE, KENTUCKY

▲ **The lupines** in New Hampshire always create a wonderful late-spring display. Their beauty has made them popular, and lots of people now come to enjoy them. On this particular day, my husband and I were the only ones around, since a light rain deterred most of the tourists, the locals and even the bugs.

Lisa Cuchara
HAMDEN, CONNECTICUT

► **I always walk** through my flower garden each morning, and it brings me joy to observe what is blooming. One morning, this clematis had opened and raindrops were sitting on its petals! Seeing the beautiful bloom covered in raindrops was like renewal to my soul that day.

Sheri Todd
BRUNDIDGE, ALABAMA

While on vacation

in Florida, I spotted these gorgeous flowers at Marie Selby Botanical Gardens in Sarasota. I eventually found out the plant is called a blue sky thunbergia vine. I love the way the blooms look with the sky behind them.

Robin Leja
PICKERINGTON, OHIO

Growing Lingo

Easy-to-understand definitions of 13 common gardening terms.

Harvest lettuce before it bolts, which is when it starts to produce seeds.

A gardener snips wayward deutzia branches. Wait for spring flowers to fade before doing a complete prune.

WHETHER YOU ARE just beginning or you've been in the garden for decades, give yourself a refresher on some common terms. The next time you chat with a garden center employee or a neighbor over the back fence, you'll sound like a pro.

ANNUAL VS. PERENNIAL.
It may seem logical that an annual plant comes back annually. But that would be a perennial, as in a perennial star year after year. An annual blooms, goes to seed and dies all in one growing season—in other words, it needs to regenerate itself annually.

BIENNIAL refers to a plant that sprouts one year, flowers the next and then dies.

BOLTING is another way of saying "going to seed." Lettuce plants bolt as hot weather sets in. Sensing their time is short, they hurriedly form seed for the next generation.

COVER CROPS are crops that are sowed quickly to cover the soil and protect it from erosion. Later, the crops are turned into the soil to release nutrients.

DEADHEADING is removing old flowers after they wilt. This encourages new blooms and keeps the plant from going to seed.

DETERMINATE VS. INDETERMINATE.
A determinate plant has a predetermined size, at which point it stops growing. An indeterminate plant has a less definite mature size—it grows until something stops it, such as a barrier or a fall frost.

GROWING MEDIUM is a sweeping term describing whatever a plant is growing in—whether it's topsoil, potting mix or compost.

HARDENING OFF is when a gardener gradually transitions tender plants to the outdoors by slowly introducing them to wind and direct sunlight until they adjust to their new surroundings.

PRUNING VS. PINCHING.
Pruning is the purposeful removal of unwanted growth, perhaps by using hand pruners to cut back a stem or a chainsaw to remove a limb. Pinching is a form of pruning during which part of the stem tip is removed near a node to encourage side branching.

SCARIFICATION VS. STRATIFICATION.
These are two different treatments to get seeds to sprout. Scarification is nicking the outer coat, while stratification is subjecting the seed to cold for a period of time, mimicking winter.

TOP DRESSING simply means topping off the soil with up to an inch of fertilizer, compost or other soil amendment to replenish the area and aid growth.

VOLUNTEERS are those plants that sprout on their own without the intervention of people, whether they come from acorns squirrels left or seeds dropping on bare soil.

XERISCAPING is landscaping that features plants which tolerate drought and need little irrigation.

CHAPTER 6

Butterfly Life

Enjoy gorgeous photos and learn what really draws in these delicate fliers.

Fluttering Through Summer

A flawless butterfly picture is hard to capture, but *Birds & Blooms* readers nailed these lucky shots.

I took this photo of a clouded sulphur on a cosmos at my parents' farm in western Kentucky on the Fourth of July. I used my Canon PowerShot SX60 HS to capture the bright, happy yellows.

Kim Enoch
KNOXVILLE, TENNESSEE

I planted milkweed after learning about the importance of saving our pollinators. I could not believe my eyes when I saw so many butterflies, especially monarchs, visiting the flowers every day! Using my Canon EOS Rebel T5i camera, I took this photo of two monarchs enjoying the blossoms on a warm summer morning.

Raven Ouellette
SUDBURY, ONTARIO

► I was on a trip in Montreal, Quebec, with my mom when I took this photo of a painted lady in a gorgeous garden. I love taking pictures of nature. Anytime I can capture this type of beauty, it is a special moment for me.

Kim Pease
BROOKFIELD, WISCONSIN

▼ My brother knew

I was going to visit him in North Carolina in October, and he planted zinnias to surround his porch so I could see all the birds and butterflies while I was there. I spotted many types of butterflies around his house, but it was a treat to see a fiery skipper. My brother always treats me like a queen, and looking at the photos I took at his home brings back memories of all the good times we had.

Gail Jakubiak
HUDSON, FLORIDA

▲ **Last summer** I decided to plant several flowers native to Pennsylvania. The flowers attracted an abundance of butterflies and bees. I would go out each day to garden and to photograph the wildlife with my Nikon COOLPIX P900. This orange sulfur butterfly caught my eye because it matched the flowers.

Nancy Tully
EAST STROUDSBURG, PENNSYLVANIA

► **As a gift,** my son and daughter-in-law took me to the Desert Botanical Garden in Phoenix, Arizona, where I took this photo of a white peacock butterfly drinking nectar from a daisy. It reminds me of my childhood, when I would chase after butterflies and pick wild daisies to give to my mother.

Shirley Hancock
SINKS GROVE, WEST VIRGINIA

There's a sunflower extravaganza each summer at Dewberry Farm in Kernersville, North Carolina. While wandering through the fields of 19 types of sunflowers, I snapped a photo of an eastern tiger swallowtail as it floated in front of my Canon Rebel camera.

Phylicia Clemens
LEXINGTON, NORTH CAROLINA

It was quiet by Lake Champlain in South Hero, Vermont, and the late afternoon sun was backlighting a lonely giant swallowtail. I spent quite a long time photographing it, mostly as it sat on the flowers, but I got lucky with a few flight shots, too. This photo reflects the natural beauty of Vermont. I felt fortunate to capture this wonderful, animated butterfly.

David Horak
ESSEX JUNCTION, VERMONT

► **This little** common buckeye shared a purple coneflower bloom with a bee during a warm day in July. I took this photo at the JC Raulston Arboretum in Raleigh with a Nikon D7200.

Nick Conde-Dudding
RALEIGH, NORTH CAROLINA

▼ **I call this photo** "Three's a crowd." It was really humorous to watch these European skippers fight for a position on this grass flower. It took many attempts to capture the trio with reasonable focus.

Jerry Taylor
BELGRADE, MONTANA

Total Attraction

These powerhouse blooms are top options for a wildlife-friendly garden, and butterflies especially love them.

FROM LEFT: GAP PHOTOS/NICOLA STOCKEN; GAP PHOTOS/JONATHAN BUCKLEY

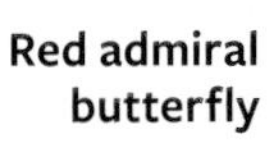

Red admiral butterfly

◄ COSMOS

COSMOS SPP., ANNUAL

Throughout the growing season, bees and butterflies can't resist these colorful pinwheel-shaped blossoms with feathery foliage. Grow single or double cultivars of this easygoing bloomer in full sun and you'll have flowers and seeds for the birds from summer through late fall. Plants stand from 1 to 6 feet high, so no matter how large your space, there's a type of cosmos that will fit right in.

► BLACK-EYED SUSAN

RUDBECKIA SPP., ZONES 3 TO 9

Lovely as a background planting or in a wildflower garden, black-eyed Susan also shines when grouped with other daisy-shaped flowers. Plants range from 1 to 6 feet in height, offering a big visual impact in just about any size yard. Butterflies appreciate the landing pad the blooms provide, bees flock to the bright yellow color and birds love the late-fall seed heads.

Female ruby-throated hummingbird at zinnia

Aphrodite fritillary on coneflower

▲ ZINNIA

ZINNIA SPP., ANNUAL

This flower is a butterfly and hummingbird garden go-to, but several varieties of sparrows, finches and juncos eat the seeds later in the year. This annual is bee-friendly, too, attracting honeybees, bumblebees and some solitary bees. It reaches up to 3 feet and blooms until the first frost.

◄ CONEFLOWER

ECHINACEA SPP., ZONES 3 TO 9

Birds, bees and butterflies, such as fritillaries, truly love this perennial! You'll watch songbirds pause to nibble the seeds, and you'll see butterflies and hummers stop to sip the nectar into fall. In winter, the remaining seed heads are an interesting garden focal point.

◄ VERBENA

VERBENA X HYBRIDA, ANNUAL TO ZONE 9

Expect summerlong color from these attractive blooms. The plant's stems spread out to about 18 inches. Keep the soil moist but well drained for optimal flowering. Verbena does well in containers, so use it to lure pollinators to small spaces.

CLOCKWISE FROM BOTTOM LEFT: BALL HORTICULTURAL COMPANY; JAMES SCHWABEL/ALAMY STOCK PHOTO;

▶ BLAZING STAR

LIATRIS SPP., ZONES 3 TO 9

The nectar of this spiky plant is a butterfly favorite, especially when it comes to the silver-spotted skipper. After the flowers fade, birds favor the seeds, which are easy to pick out in the garden. Blazing star reaches up to 6 feet tall, but some types, like Kobold, are much shorter, measuring roughly 18 inches.

▶ BEE BALM

MONARDA SPP., ZONES 3 TO 9

This unusual beauty grows up to 4 feet tall and starts flowering in midsummer, inviting hummingbirds, butterflies and bees to your flower bed. Plants come in hues of pink, red, white and purple; choose mildew resistant varieties for best results. Frequent deadheading keeps this enthusiastic self-sower in check, but then you won't see songbirds stopping by to eat the seeds once petals die back. The choice is yours!

▼ AGASTACHE

AGASTACHE SPP., ZONES 4 TO 11

Bushy and studded with blooms from mid- to late summer, agastache is a favorite of bees, hummingbirds and butterflies. Flower spires in pink, orange, yellow, blue or violet reach 2 to 6 feet high. Agastache thrives in full sun and in well-draining, fertile soil.

Honeybee on blazing star

Male ruby-throated hummingbird at bee balm

Cabbage white butterfly on agastache

Monarch on swamp milkweed (*Asclepias incarnata*)

Master Milkweed

To help monarchs, grow the one plant they need the most.

Showy milkweed

MONARCH BUTTERFLIES are rapidly declining due to loss of habitat and the use of pesticides. As gardeners mobilize, planting milkweed is the most effective way to help because it is the only plant that sustains a monarch through each of its life stages. Milkweed also produces a chemical that makes monarchs toxic and bitter-tasting to some of their predators.

"The bottom line is, if milkweed disappears, so will monarchs," says Laura Lukens, who works as a national monitoring coordinator for the Monarch Joint Venture, a partnership of American federal, state and other organizations. "Home gardeners have a huge role to play in providing habitat for monarchs, pollinators and other wildlife. Residential properties have the potential to contribute many thousands—maybe even millions—of acres of habitat."

Milkweed, scientifically called *Asclepias*, is a huge genus, with 73 species native to the United States and more than 100 species across North America. It's the only plant that hosts monarch caterpillars.

Choose Wisely

Select milkweeds native to your region. Common names vary wildly, so use botanical names when you are researching. Since milkweed species have varying needs for sun, water and space, pay extra attention to growing requirements. Find a directory of native plant vendors in the Habitat Needs tab under About Monarchs on *monarchjointventure.org*.

"We recommend planting a diversity of native milkweeds and flowering plants to provide monarchs with food throughout the entire season," Laura says.

Avoid tropical milkweed (*A. curassavica*). Although easy to grow, tropical types host a parasite that infects and harms monarchs. It may encourage monarchs to stop short of their full migration, increasing the risk of parasitic transmission. Check with native plant specialists to learn how to minimize problems year-round, such as cutting plants back to a few inches tall in fall and winter.

Get Growing

The easiest way to grow milkweed is to start with plants instead of seeds, tucking them into the ground after the danger of frost has passed.

Starting milkweed from seed is tricky. Most seeds need a period of chilling called vernalization and stratification to germinate and then flower. In cold climates, plant seeds directly into the ground in autumn. Indoors, place seeds between moist paper towels inside a sealed plastic bag or plant the seeds directly into peat pots covered with a sealed plastic bag. Chill in a refrigerator at least 30 days. Plant cold-treated seeds in a moist seed-starting potting mix. Place the pots under a grow light or near a sunny window. Warning: Seedlings may take a long time to emerge or not grow at all.

If the seedlings make it, start to transplant the 2- to 3-inch plants with the intact rootball after the danger of frost has passed. Most milkweeds have long taproots that hate to be disturbed. A seedling may lose its leaves after being transplanted, or it could die.

Some types of milkweed spread more aggressively than others. To contain the plant, grow it in a raised bed or container and remove the pods. Or plant it only where it can run freely. Milkweed does not need to be fertilized.

PREVIOUS SPREAD: MEDIA MARKETING/SHUTTERSTOCK; THIS SPREAD, LEFT: MAUREEN RUDDY BURKHART/ALAMY

Mexican whorled milkweed

Antelopehorns milkweed

Monarch caterpillars on common milkweed

BEST MILKWEEDS FOR YOUR REGION

Monarch Joint Venture recommends these regional milkweed species. Download a fact sheet at monarchjointventure.org.

NORTHEAST/MIDWEST: common (*Asclepias syriaca*); swamp (*A. incarnata*); butterfly weed (*A. tuberosa*); whorled (*A. verticillata*); poke (*A. exaltata*).

SOUTHEAST: butterfly weed (*A. tuberosa*); whorled (*A. verticillata*); white (*A. variegata*); aquatic (*A. perennis*); sandhill/pinewoods (*A. humistrata*).

SOUTH CENTRAL: green antelopehorn (*A. viridis*); antelopehorns (*A. asperula*); zizotes (*A. oenotheroides*).

WESTERN, EXCLUDING ARIZONA AND CALIFORNIA: Mexican whorled (*A. fascicularis*); showy (*A. speciosa*).

ARIZONA: butterfly weed (*A. tuberosa*); antelopehorns (*A. asperula*); rush (*A. subulata*); Arizona (*A. angustifolia*).

CALIFORNIA: Mexican whorled (*A. fascicularis*); showy (*A. speciosa*); desert (*A. erosa*); California (*A. californica*); heartleaf (*A. cordifolia*); woolly (*A. vestita*); woolly pod (*A. eriocarpa*).

Good to Know Before You Grow

Wear gloves when handling milkweed, because the milky sap may cause skin or eye irritation. In large quantities, the sap may be toxic to livestock or pets.

Milkweed may attract aphids and other insects. "While a high concentration of aphids on your milkweed may look bad, these insects are not necessarily causing harm to monarchs," Laura says. "Unless they are in extremely high density, there are usually not enough to kill the plant."

Because chemical pesticides or insecticides also kill monarchs, the best option is to remove the pests by hand, cut off stems with lots of aphids or simply allow nature to take its course.

Butterfly weed

A monarch butterfly pauses on a purple coneflower bloom.

Plant the Perfect Paradise

Grow your own wildflowers and watch for fluttering wings and gentle landings.

PICTURE A MEADOW full of colorful wildflowers swaying in the breeze, while butterflies float among them under the warm summer sun. It sounds like a lovely dream. Now, imagine that idyllic scene in your own backyard. It takes some effort to start, but creating a wildflower garden for butterflies is very rewarding—and easier than you'd think.

Why Wildflowers

Butterflies and wildflowers have evolved together into a perfect relationship over the years. The wildflowers bloom at different times, emerging as butterflies begin to feed and breed in spring, and dying off as winged beauties migrate south or begin hibernation. In return, the butterflies pollinate the plants as they travel through.

Create a Haven

Whether you want a few square feet or a whole meadow, here's how to grow a wildflower wonderland.

Choose a site. Wildflowers prefer gobs of sun, but a mix of morning light and afternoon shade works well, too. Make sure to consider water needs, and keep seeds well hydrated as they grow.

Prep the area. Wildflowers need to hold their own against weeds. Give them a head start by clearing all sod and other vegetation. Try covering the area with some plastic sheeting or newspaper for a month or two to allow existing greenery to die. This easy removal method doesn't require herbicides.

Research the best time to plant your seeds. Loosen the soil to a depth of 2 to 3 inches. Mix seeds with sand to easily distribute them evenly. Sow the seeds, then rake gently to cover. Water the area and cover with straw to protect seeds from hungry birds.

Watch for grass and other invaders in the first year, and weed by hand only if it is needed. As the wildflowers establish, they'll grow densely and keep most of the weeds out. Plants will bloom in the second year and drop their seeds each autumn, reseeding another generation of wildflowers.

Best Buds

These seven wildflower picks are popular among many butterfly species and thrive in almost any region of the country. Choose flowers native to your area. For more information, visit *wildflower.org* or contact your local county extension office for regional advice.

1

1. PURPLE CONEFLOWER

ECHINACEA SPP.

These tall, proud perennials are beloved as cut flowers, but be sure to leave some for the butterflies! Deadhead often to encourage new blooms, especially early in the summer.

2. SUNFLOWER

HELIANTHUS SPP.

When you think about this beloved wildflower, you probably think of common sunflower (*H. annuus*), native to the West and grown all over the country. But there are many other members of this family, like the western sunflower (*H. occidentalis*), which is perfectly suited to containers or tiny plots.

3. ASTER

SYMPHYOTRICHUM SPP.

Fringed aster flowers help extend butterfly season well into fall. Some butterflies overwinter in the North and need nectar flowers right up until the first frost. Most asters prefer sun, but some tolerate a little bit of shade, so plant in a bright spot.

4. GOLDENROD

SOLIDAGO SPP.

Ignore the common myth that goldenrod makes you sneeze. (That's likely just ragweed, which usually blooms at the same time.) These slender gold spears are another fall favorite for butterflies. Smaller-size varieties like Ohio goldenrod (*S. ohioensis*) are ideal for compact gardens.

REGIONAL ROUNDUP

NORTHEAST: New England aster (*Symphyotrichum novae-angliae*); red columbine (*Aquilegia canadensis*); bee balm (*Monarda fistulosa*).

SOUTHEAST: Purple passionflower (*Passiflora incarnata*); scarlet sage (*Salvia coccinea*); giant ironweed (*Vernonia gigantea*).

MIDWEST: Scarlet bee balm (*Monarda didyma*); Eastern smooth beardtongue (*Penstemon laevigatus*); black-eyed Susan (*Rudbeckia hirta*).

CENTRAL PLAINS: Tahoka daisy (*Machaeranthera tanacetifolia*); plains coreopsis (*Coreopsis tinctoria*); butterfly weed (*Asclepias tuberosa*).

NORTHWEST: Meadow checkermallow (*Sidalcea campestris*); blue gilia (*Gilia capitata*); Pacific aster (*Symphyotrichum chilense*).

SOUTHWEST: Mexican hat (*Ratibida columnifera*); California poppy (*Eschscholzia californica*); showy milkweed (*Asclepias speciosa*).

5. MILKWEED

ASCLEPIAS SPP.

Monarchs need milkweed, but many other butterfly species extract nectar from this wide-spread wildflower, too. Common milkweed (*A. syriaca*) grows well in much of the country, but seek out other natives if you're in the West or Southeast.

6. WILD VIOLET

VIOLA SPP.

These petite but assertive blossoms are often considered a pest in lawns and cultivated gardens. Don't root them out altogether, though. Wild violets serve as host plants for many fritillary butterfly caterpillars. Let the plants spread in your wildflower garden and look out for little spiky, but harmless, caterpillars chewing on low leaves and purple blooms.

7. BLACK-EYED SUSAN

RUDBECKIA SPP.

Rudbeckias are members of the coneflower family, with black-eyed Susans (*R. hirta*) being the most well known. But there are many other native species worth growing. These sturdy stalwarts are biennial, waiting to bloom the second year after planting from seed.

The Best Butterfly Magnets

Birds & Blooms readers share their go-to flowers for attracting pollinators.

Cloudless sulphur on lantana

When my tall verbena is in full bloom, it is like a butterfly magnet.

Teresa Wayne
PHILLIPS, NEBRASKA

I have photographed long-tailed skippers, monarchs, moths, giant swallowtails, cloudless sulphurs and gulf fritillaries getting nectar from my orange and yellow lantana flowers.

Becky A. Litke
PANAMA CITY, FLORIDA

I have planted many flowers in my yard to attract butterflies, including milkweed to help monarchs, and four lilac bushes.

Clarice McKenney
BONNERS FERRY, IDAHO

I have an herb garden outside my kitchen window that includes Joe Pye weed. Last summer, eastern tiger swallowtails visited it on a daily basis.

Lyn Cosby
ATLANTA, GEORGIA

The phlox in our yard never fails to attract butterflies, particularly swallowtails. We have several containers of pink and purple phlox that bloom every summer.

Jim Thomas
SUBLIMITY, OREGON

Our sedum is what we watch every year for pollinators, including butterflies.

Anne Veldhuisen
MARSHALL, MINNESOTA

Eastern tiger swallowtail on butterfly weed

Garden Royalty

Soar through the fascinating world of monarch butterflies.

A monarch searches for nectar on a zinnia flower.

1 Monarchs don't need a GPS to locate their migration destination. Many of the gorgeous travelers find their way to the same exact location, perhaps even to one particular tree, where previous generations have wintered before.

3 Don't be fooled! There are three other butterflies that look very similar to monarchs: soldiers, queens and viceroys.

55 In order for these delicate creatures to fly, their wing muscles must stay above 55 degrees Fahrenheit.

12 It's all about speed! The travelers flap their wings up to 12 times a second when flying at their fastest.

2 Male and female monarchs look very similar, but the males have two dark spots on their hindwings that females do not.

500

A female monarch in the wild can lay up to 500 eggs throughout her lifetime, and in captivity female butterflies are able to lay even more.

Monarch laying eggs

These amber beauties could fly circles around other species. During fall migration, they travel farther than any other tropical butterfly—up to 3,000 miles.

Best Dressed

Host a gala for elegant zebra swallowtails by growing their favorite nectar plants.

CATERPILLAR: KEVIN COLLISON/SHUTTERSTOCK

A red spot at the base of the wings creates a place for predators to aim away from the tiny body, increasing chances of survival.

▲ **I see mostly** tiger swallowtails in my yard, but this zebra swallowtail showed up one day! It was exciting to see a new species.

Susan Perren
FREDERICKSBURG, VIRGINIA

◄ **The zebra swallowtail** is Tennessee's state butterfly, but we rarely see them in the western part of the state. It was such a thrill to find one so I took photos of the whole life cycle. Rare, indeed!

Jean Owens
PARIS, TENNESSEE

Zebra swallowtail caterpillars vary in color. Some are mostly green, while others are greenish or black with yellow stripes.

ZEBRA SWALLOWTAIL

WINGSPAN

2½ to 4 inches.

DISTINCTIVE MARKINGS

Wings have bold black stripes on a white or teal-white background. Hindwings feature a red stripe on the underside and a lengthy tail.

HABITAT

Typically inhabits wide-open areas to feed. To breed, it travels to wooded spaces around swamps and rivers.

HOST PLANTS

Prefers the pawpaw tree or others in its genus.

BACKYARD FAVORITES

Enjoys nectar from blueberry, blackberry, lilac, redbud and milkweed.

Salute the Admiral

Watch for these majestic beauties to sail into your backyard.

RED ADMIRAL

WINGSPAN

1¾ to 2½ inches.

DISTINCTIVE MARKINGS

The forewing is dark with a red-orange stripe and white dots, and the hindwing boasts a red-orange border.

HABITAT

Found nearly everywhere. Males are especially active in the afternoon and evening as they look for females.

HOST PLANTS

Nettles—stinging nettle, false nettle, wood nettle.

NECTAR FAVORITES

Adults visit flowers but prefer tree sap, fermenting fruit and animal droppings.

RANGE

United States, Mexico and southern Canada, plus Europe and western Asia.

▲ **A red admiral** caught my interest with its tapestry of color. I watched it go from one flower to another and patiently waited for it to come closer. It finally landed a few feet away from me. The light from behind made the edges of its wings glow and the blues look luminous.

Michelle Nyss
MILWAUKEE, WISCONSIN

◀ **This plum tree's** sweet fragrance alone was breathtaking, but the red admiral made the scene in my parents' backyard even better.

Ursula Anderson
HINES, MINNESOTA

Caterpillars are black or dark brown, with or without speckling, and have yellow side markings.

Works of Art

There's more to intricately patterned painted ladies than meets the eye.

PAINTED LADY

WINGSPAN

2 to 2⅞ inches.

DISTINCTIVE MARKINGS

Orange and black patterned upper wing with white dots and four or five black dots along each hindwing. Underwings have a dark brown and tan segmented design with four or five dots on the hindwing's edge.

HABITAT

Found in nearly every habitat, but prefers open grassy areas, gardens and fields.

HOST PLANTS

Uses a variety of host plants (more than 100), but prefers thistle, hollyhock, mallow and many legumes.

BACKYARD FAVORITES

Nectar from thistle, aster, cosmos, ironweed and blazing star.

ZOOMING ALONG

Painted ladies are fast fliers, fluttering at speeds of up to 25 mph.

▲ **This painted lady** landed on a frog! I didn't notice it when I first took the picture. I almost deleted it from my computer, but I was astounded when I saw the frog. When will I see anything like this again? Probably never.

Charles Miller
MINNEAPOLIS, MINNESOTA

◀ **While out in the garden** with my then 5-year-old daughter, we spotted this beautiful painted lady on one of our sunflowers. This image is so special because it reminds me of the moments my children and I share in our garden.

Catherine Pouria
STOCKTON, NEW JERSEY

Painted lady caterpillars are gray-brown or almost black with a yellow stripe down their bodies and spikes along their sides and backs. They show some color variation when in caterpillar stage. Before the pupae stage, look for caterpillars creating silk tents on thistle, one of their favorite host plants.

Search for Silver

Welcome silver-spotted skippers with the flower nectar they prefer.

▲ **This skipper** was enjoying a coneflower in my garden. I love how its eye looks almost as if it's made of glass or marble.

Christine Gill
MARICOPA, ARIZONA

► **I noticed some** butterflies at our flowers while I was mowing the lawn, so I ran and got my camera. They had all flown away when I returned, except for this lone skipper. I waited for it to land for nectar.

Michael Nanton
CAMILLUS, NEW YORK

◄ **A silver-spotted** skipper stopped to enjoy the sweet William flowers in my neighbor's yard. It was a beautiful scene that I happened upon while out on a walk one day.

Kathy Jenkins
ALBRIGHT, WEST VIRGINIA

A yellow body and a brown-red head with bold eye spots help a skipper caterpillar stand out.

SILVER-SPOTTED SKIPPER

WINGSPAN

1¾ to 2¼ inches.

DISTINCTIVE MARKINGS

Upperside of the wings is dark brown with a long golden orange section toward the center. Hindwings have a prominent silver-white spot.

RANGE

Most of the continental U.S. and southern Canada.

HABITAT

Roadsides, gardens, fields and woodland edges.

HOST PLANTS

Black locust, false indigo, American wisteria and honey locust.

EGGS

Females lay single green (sometimes appearing white) eggs on or near host plants.

NECTAR FAVORITES

Common milkweed, blazing star and thistles.

Pearl of the Garden

Plant some asters and watch these crescents raise their broods.

PEARL CRESCENT

WINGSPAN

About 1¼ inches.

DISTINCTIVE MARKINGS

The upperside of each wing is orange with large black patches and stripes. A small, pale crescent moon-shaped marking is on the underside of each hindwing.

RANGE

Most of the U.S. east of the Rockies and parts of southern Canada.

HABITAT

Gardens, fields, roadsides and near woodlands.

HOST PLANTS

Many types of asters.

EGGS

Adults lay minuscule white-green eggs in clusters on host plants.

NECTAR FAVORITES

Asters are your best bet for attracting pearl crescents, but they'll visit almost any butterfly favorite.

◄ **This little guy** visits the vibrant sunflowers growing beneath a window in my front yard nearly every day. I grew the blooms from seeds saved many years ago from my grandmother's garden.

Amy Doza
MEMPHIS, TENNESSEE

▲ **A friend gave me** a few asters several years ago. The purple blooms attracted this bright pearl crescent.

Paul Hogsett
HALIFAX, PENNSYLVANIA

► **I love how** the dark background allows the colors of this photo to stand out. It made my day when this pearl crescent stayed on the bloom for such a long time! I got several good pictures.

Maria Brueggemann
INDEPENDENCE, KENTUCKY

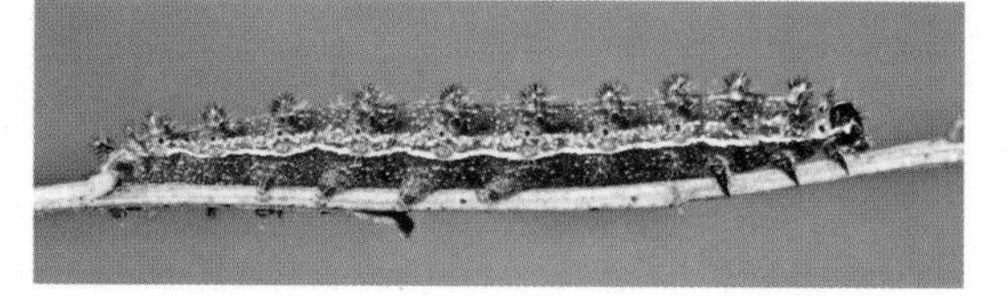

Mostly brown with a cream stripe down the side, pearl crescent caterpillars have many small spikes.

Bow to the Queen

Share your milkweed with these regal year-round southern residents.

▲ **We love when our** Mexican sunflower blooms, because our butterfly population is best then—especially the queens.

Janet Christensen
ORACLE, ARIZONA

► **I saw this beautiful** queen butterfly on a bush when my husband and I traveled to the Mojave Desert. I love the contrast between its rusty color and the yellow chaparral plant.

Deborah Saldana
OAK HILLS, CALIFORNIA

◄ **I watched** this queen butterfly hatch from its chrysalis. What a perfect color combination with my yellow hibiscus!

Loradel Herringshaw
LAKE CITY, FLORIDA

Queen caterpillars have black and white stripes and yellow accents, much like monarchs. Queens have three sets of protuberances, but monarchs have only two.

QUEEN

WINGSPAN

2½ to 4 inches.

DISTINCTIVE MARKINGS

Underwings resemble a monarch's, with white outlines on black hindwing veins and dark borders featuring white dots. Orange forewings have white specks.

HABITAT

Open, sunny areas with flowers, including fields, deserts, roadsides and pastures.

HOST PLANT

Milkweed or milkweed vines.

NECTAR FAVORITES

Adults sip from many flowers, including fogfruit and shepherd's needle.

QUIRKY QUALITY

Several adult queens may gather on the same plant to roost overnight, although there's no obvious reason why.

Border Butterflies

Blue metalmark

South Texas offers a look at diverse species found nowhere else in the Lower 48.

Two-barred flasher

SOUTH TEXAS IS WELL documented for tropical bird diversity—known for green jays and great kiskadees—but butterflies of the region also reflect a southern influence. If you want to see a blue metalmark, pavon emperor or white-striped longtail, you'll need to head for the border.

FLUTTERING SPECIES DIVERSITY

The Lower Rio Grande Valley, a three-county region at the southern tip of Texas, is home to 300 butterfly species, including nearly 100 not found any farther north. People travel to this tropical region for a chance to see rare gems such as crimson patches, Mexican bluewings and two-barred flashers.

According to Marianna Trevino-Wright, director of the National Butterfly Center near Mission, Texas, "We've observed 240 species of butterflies and 286 species of birds on our 100 acres." She says, "It is easy to rack up lots of observations in a short visit."

Butterfly-watching is an excellent social activity. Butterflies aren't as easily spooked as birds. Photographers find the hobby particularly rewarding, especially on cooler mornings when the flutterers are less active. Before the sun dries the early dew, many butterflies will bask with "wings spread out like solar panels," Marianna says.

BEYOND THE GARDENS

The National Butterfly Center has an "if you plant it, they will come" philosophy. "People always ask why we have such a great volume and diversity of butterflies," Marianna says. "Well, it's because we bait them. By providing both their preferred nectar and host plants, we sort of lure them in."

Butterflies are found in the gardens, but they also flit about the prairie and forest landscapes. Some feed on grass pollen; others key in on tree sap. Many get nutrients from animal waste. Butterflies are also reliant on their host plants, from which males patrol in search of mates and where females lay eggs.

ALL DAY, ANY DAY

The early bird may get the worm, but butterflies prefer the brunch hour. Butterfly-viewing heats up in midmorning. The stunning insects are most active under sunny skies and temperatures above 70 degrees Fahrenheit. The evening roost period also can be productive for butterfly seekers. Marianna suggests looking for clusters of zebra heliconians roosting together.

While in South Texas, butterflies are found any day of the year, they will appear in booms, responding to bursts of flowers after rainfall events. During March, October and November, consistent action is likely, but drought can impact this. There really is no wrong day to visit the borderlands of South Texas.

SOUTH TEXAS HOT SPOTS

The Lower Rio Grande Valley is a fertile hub for agricultural production. Viewing nature is best in patches of protected lands. Together these parcels create a corridor of wildlife habitat along the river's flood plain and preserve 11 ecosystems, including tidal wetlands and brushland scrub. The North American Butterfly Association has an extensive list of regional hot spots, with the following as highlights.

NATIONAL BUTTERFLY CENTER

A project of the North American Butterfly Association, the center hosts the Texas Butterfly Festival each fall. Bentsen-Rio Grande Valley State Park is just up the road and worth a visit, too.

SABAL PALM SANCTUARY

Numerous butterfly gardens make this a top destination. Beyond the gardens, the center has trails through a variety of habitats.

LAGUNA ATASCOSA, SANTA ANA AND LOWER RIO GRANDE VALLEY NATIONAL WILDLIFE REFUGES

The U.S. Fish and Wildlife Service administers a number of refuges in the region to provide extensive habitat for a variety of wildlife, from alligators to ocelots.

CHAPTER 7

Ask the Experts

Get answers to birding and gardening questions from pros Kenn and Kimberly Kaufman and Melinda Myers.

I saw this chipping sparrow feed a much larger baby bird. Is it common for birds to feed other species?

Julia Worth
WEYMOUTH, MASSACHUSETTS

Kenn and Kimberly: You've witnessed an odd relationship in the bird world: the result of brood parasitism by a brown-headed cowbird. Cowbirds don't build nests or tend to their own young. They employ what seems to be an unfair strategy of laying eggs in the nests of other birds, such as this chipping sparrow. The adoptive adults care for the young, unaware they aren't its biological parents. It can be tough to see a small songbird feeding the much larger young cowbird, but it's very important not to interfere. Cowbirds are a native species, protected by law. They do create conservation challenges for some species, such as Kirtland's warbler, but in general nature manages to maintain a fair balance.

How do I make my backyard both dog- and bird-friendly?

Susan Miller MILWAUKEE, WISCONSIN

Kenn and Kimberly: The good news is that making a yard safe for dogs also makes it safer for you, your family and the birds. The most important thing gardeners can do is avoid treating their lawns with chemicals. Recent studies indicate a correlation between lawn chemicals and cancer in canines. These chemicals can also harm insects and the birds that feed on them. Embrace the idea of a less-treated lawn to benefit all living creatures.

PUPPY: JLSNADER/SHUTTERSTOCK; FEEDER: STUART MONK/SHUTTERSTOCK

Female ruby-throated hummingbirds

Q Should I add anything to the sugar water for my hummingbirds to make it more nutritious?

Roger Emerick
SOUTH GLASTONBURY, CONNECTICUT

Kenn and Kimberly: Hummingbirds drink nectar and sugar water for energy. When you're feeding them pure sugar water, there's no need to put in additives. These birds forage at other sources besides feeders, getting plenty of nutrition from eating small insects like flies and gnats. They even eat small spiders. And hummingbirds are so resourceful that they often forage for insects in the sap wells drilled in trees by sapsuckers.

Q I cut down most of the black walnut trees near my garden, added topsoil and rototilled, but my plants still wilt. What should I do next?

Sarah Tims SPRINGFIELD CENTER, NEW YORK

Melinda: It takes at least five years for the roots, leaf litter and nut husks of black walnut trees to decompose fully and no longer pose a threat to susceptible plants. The roots of the remaining black walnuts can spread several hundred feet away from the trunk of the tree. As your new plantings mature and their roots grow, they may come in contact with remaining tree remnants or the roots of existing trees. Time will take care of the debris from removed trees. For now, consider growing resistant plants—you can find examples on extension office, university or arboreta websites. Or grow plants in raised beds lined with landscape fabric to prevent black walnut roots from invading the garden.

ADEPT BUILDER

Sometime around May, female Baltimore orioles use straw, grass, bark, animal fur and other materials to create elaborate hanging nests.

Q When is the best time to put out nesting materials for birds?

Sharon Day
EAST KINGSTON, NEW HAMPSHIRE

Kenn and Kimberly: Birds gather materials to line their nests at various times of the year—including fall, when they make shelters for roosting during the winter—but most nest building is in spring and early summer. In your area of New Hampshire, eastern bluebirds and house finches might begin to build nests as early as the end of March, so that would be a good time to start if you have lots of material to offer. If you want to wait for the peak season, start at the end of April.

Q What ground covers tolerate sun and shade and are tough enough to handle traffic from two dogs?

Joy Chanin MARIETTA, GEORGIA

Melinda: Many dog owners have given up on growing ground covers in areas where their dogs dig and play. Artificial turf may not be your first choice, but it may be the only green option. Wood chip mulch can create a parklike setting. Just be sure the chips are a size and shape that's safe for your dogs—check with your veterinarian first. Consider building a few raised-bed gardens that will provide planting space that's less accessible to dogs.

Q An albino hummingbird came to visit. How rare are birds like this?

David Jones MUSKOGEE, OKLAHOMA

Kenn and Kimberly: Every year there are a few reports of hummingbirds that are partly or mostly white. These birds lack most of the melanin and other pigments in their feathers and are called leucistic. But the bird in your photo appears to have the characteristics of a true albino: completely white feathers, pink bill and feet, and even pink eyes. Such true albinos are extremely rare. What a treat to have this exceptional and beautiful bird visiting your feeders.

Q The leaves on my lilac curl up and it has never fully flowered. What might be wrong?

Susan Hartzell SOUTH LAKE TAHOE, CALIFORNIA

Melinda: Lilac blight caused by bacteria may lead to curling leaves. Brown blemishes or lesions may appear on the leaves and new shoots. Pruning out infected branches below the diseased portion is the only control. Be sure to disinfect your tools with alcohol or a disinfectant spray between cuts. If leaves are curled but green and free of spots, it may be a root issue caused by too much or not enough water. Try watering thoroughly and less often to encourage deep roots. Insufficient sunlight, overfertilization or pruning any time other than right after the lilac flowers (or when it should have flowered) can prevent it from blooming the next year.

Q This woodpecker visits our feeders. What species is it?

Scott and Jean DeGolier WAUNAKEE, WISCONSIN

Kenn and Kimberly: Every once in a while a birder is lucky enough to see a truly unique individual; this is such a bird. It's a downy woodpecker, but one with an odd condition affecting its plumage. The feathers that ordinarily would be black are a light brownish gray, apparently because the melanin pigments in those feathers are reduced. In technical terms, this would be called either leucistic or dilute plumage. Although birds with odd-colored feathers look distinctly unusual, they often lead healthy lives, finding mates and raising young just as most normally colored individuals do.

Q I found two hummingbird nests in my tree. Do they reuse their nests or build new ones?

Kriss Reiff GRAND JUNCTION, COLORADO

Kenn and Kimberly: A hummingbird nest is a tiny marvel. Female hummingbirds use the finest plant fibers and spiderwebs to craft a secure cradle for eggs and young. It is strong for its size, but such a nest is not durable enough for repeated use. Typically, the female will build a new nest for each brood, even within the same year. She may start construction before she finishes feeding the full-grown young from a previous one. In rare cases, a location is so good that females build right on top of the remains of an old nest.

Q I grew this bulb a relative gave to me—what kind of plant is it?

Stephanie Byrd
FORT GIBSON, OKLAHOMA

Melinda: You might be surprised to discover that your family member gave you a type of daffodil (*Narcissus*). Your daffodil variety, Cheerfulness, is just one of many that differ greatly from the traditional yellow daffodil. The double flowers of Cheerfulness are fragrant and appear in late spring. Its heat tolerance makes it a smart choice for gardeners in warmer regions like yours.

HUMMINGBIRD: ELSIE JONES; BLACKBIRD: WILLIAM LEAMAN

MARSH SINGERS

Listen for male red-winged blackbirds in wetland areas. They perch on tall vegetation and belt out *conk-la-ree*!

Q I'm curious, why do birds sing after a storm?

Lori Sheldon BORGER, TEXAS

Kenn and Kimberly: After a storm, especially a bad one, it's reassuring to hear birds singing. It's mostly male birds that sing. They tune up after storms for the same reasons that they belt out songs early in the morning. Each male sings to announce his claim to a territory—the area that he defends for raising a family—and to communicate with his mate. So at dawn's first light, or as soon as the storm passes, the message in his song is "I'm still here." It reassures his mate that he's guarding the territory and lets neighboring males know that this turf is still occupied.

Q Should I remove the burlap wrap before I plant a new tree?

MaryAnne Katz PORTLAND, OREGON

Melinda: There's a great deal of debate among arborists and other growers as to whether you should keep or remove the burlap. Some nurseries void their guarantee if you remove the burlap at planting. Always remove treated burlap that does not decay in the soil. I have removed planted trees where the burlap and wire cages were fully intact. So I prefer to cut away the burlap wrap and wire cages once the tree is settled in the planting hole. This minimizes disturbances of the rootball while you are removing the materials. Minimally, you should remove the twine and peel back the burlap so it is not exposed to the air. Burlap acts like a wick, moving moisture from the soil surrounding the tree roots to the surface, where it evaporates into the air.

Q My bougainvillea bush is doing great but doesn't flower. What's going on?

Peter Grant CRYSTAL RIVER, FLORIDA

Melinda: Too much shade, water, nitrogen fertilizer and pruning can all reduce or prevent flowering. Overwatering can negatively impact bougainvilleas that are native to arid locations. Excess nitrogen encourages leaf and stem growth at the expense of flowers. Overpruning or pruning at the wrong time can eliminate flower buds. Prune right after the plants finish flowering if you need to control their sizes and shapes.

Q I saw a ruby-throated hummingbird trying to get nectar from a dandelion. Is that normal?

Kris Brown KAUKAUNA, WISCONSIN

Kenn and Kimberly: Like most other hummingbirds, ruby-throats typically seek out long, tube-shaped flowers—they're especially attracted to red ones. Dandelion blooms—flat and yellow—don't fit the usual profile. But ruby-throated hummingbirds have to be more adaptable than many other hummingbirds because they migrate such a long distance through different habitats, dealing with big variations in weather and climate. It's an advantage for them to be flexible and to check out whatever flowers are available. Dandelions do contain some nectar, so it's not necessarily a waste of effort for the bird.

Q Is it OK to bake birdseed so it doesn't sprout?

Alice Ritchie
SALISBURY, NORTH CAROLINA

Kenn and Kimberly: For keeping things tidy in a garden, baking is one way to sterilize seeds and cut down on weeds. Different approaches work, but the most common suggestion is to spread out birdseed on a baking sheet in a layer less than an inch deep and bake at 300 degrees for 20 to 30 minutes. Five minutes in a microwave may be just as effective. You can experiment with variations of these methods. As long as you don't burn the seeds, you can't go wrong. Note: Chopped sunflower hearts won't germinate, and imported Nyjer seed is usually sterilized.

Q Can I use hose water to fill birdbaths, or is the PVC harmful for birds?

Tobias Morse MONTAGUE, MICHIGAN

Kenn and Kimberly: It is true that ordinary garden hoses contain chemicals that could be harmful to birds. Besides PVC (polyvinyl chloride), the hose may contain lead or other toxins. Small amounts may leach into the water, especially when water sits in the hose for hours or days. If you're in a situation where the only practical way to fill your birdbath is with a garden hose, let the water run for at least a few minutes to wash out most of the contaminants. It's also possible to buy hoses made of safer materials; look for those labeled as being safe for drinking water.

Q I saw this hawk in the woods near my house. What species is it?

Sheryl Fleming HOFFMEISTER, NEW YORK

Kenn and Kimberly: It's a special treat to get a good look at this bird. The brown back and the wide black and white bands across the tail mark this as an adult broad-winged hawk. Unlike the red-tailed hawks that can be seen in open country and along roadsides all year, broad-winged hawks are forest birds. They're often hard to approach. In summer, they live in wooded regions of the eastern United States and Canada, mostly east of the Rockies. In fall, they migrate to the tropics, going as far south as South America.

Q What are these pretty white flowers?

Tom and Linda Christie OWL'S HEAD, MAINE

Melinda: The native little bluets (*Houstonia caerulea*) found a home in your lawn. You may also find these small but showy spring flowers growing in fields, along roadsides, in forests, near shorelines and high in the mountains. The flowers may be blue, or white like yours, with a yellow center. These plants prefer full sun or partial shade and moist, slightly acidic soil.

Q My Meyer lemon tree sprouted this odd fruit. How do I fix it?

Dan Solomon CHICO, CALIFORNIA

Melinda: Follow the stem that produced the giant fruit down to the base of the plant. It is likely a sprout from the rootstock. Ornamental and edible trees are often grafted onto the roots of another plant for increased hardiness or disease resistance, or to control the plant's size. Remove the sucker to direct all the plant's energy to the Meyer lemon instead of this sprout, which could eventually overtake your desirable plant.

Q What are these red bugs, and can they harm my butterfly weeds?

Nancy Dietrich DUNDALK, MARYLAND

Melinda: These insects are milkweed bugs in their immature stage. Adults are flatter, more elongated, and orange and black, resembling a boxelder bug. The immature bugs feed on the plant's sap and seeds. To get at the sap, they inject a chemical into the plant tissue. This liquefies the tissue, allowing them to suck it up. They don't cause significant harm to plants, but gardeners in warmer areas, where the bugs may overwinter, can remove leaf litter and spent stalks to help reduce next year's population.

BUTTERFLY: RJH_IMAGES/ALAMY STOCK PHOTO

Q In fall of 2018, my area was affected by wildfires. The next spring, thousands of painted lady butterflies migrated through. Are the events related?

Hilary Calce
THOUSAND OAKS, CALIFORNIA

Kenn and Kimberly: These massive movements of painted lady butterflies happen only occasionally, but they can be spectacular. They're not as predictable as the migration of monarch butterflies, though. The painted ladies build up huge populations and then stage these massive flights only when the rains have been exactly right for the growth of the plants their caterpillars eat—in this case, probably a variety of annuals coming up in late winter. It's possible that many of these plants came up in the areas that had burned in the fall, but the timing also could be just a coincidence.

Eastern tiger swallowtail on woodland phlox

Q Do any types of shade tolerant plants attract butterflies?

Adrianne Long
FREDERICK, MARYLAND

Melinda: You may be surprised to find a variety of native plants that tolerate shade and support butterflies. Always be sure to match the plant to the level of shade in your garden. Here are a few woodland natives to try. Start the season with Virginia bluebells, mixing them with other perennials to mask the large leaves that die back soon after flowering. Wild geraniums (*Geranium maculatum*), rose pink to lavender, appear during the cooler months in spring. Woodland phlox, with bluish flowers, appear in late spring. Foam flowers (*Tiarella cordifolia*) produce spikes of white flowers, and their foliage remains attractive all season long, even evergreen where winters are mild. Add a spark of color with the red and yellow blooms of Indian pinks, move on to the stately blooms of black cohosh (*Actaea racemosa*) and finish up the season with native turtleheads.

BUTTERFLY: KEVIN COLLISON/SHUTTERSTOCK

Q Should I move my jade plant to a bigger pot?

Sandy Crooms CLARKESVILLE, GEORGIA

Melinda: Cacti and succulents have relatively small root systems for the size of the growth above ground. Moving a plant too often or keeping it in a container too big can result in the potting mix staying wet, leading to root rot. It's time to transplant when the roots begin to encircle the rootball or new growth is stunted. Your plant (below) appears to be thriving, but it looks as if it's settled in the container. This is not a problem. Some gardeners prefer to adjust this by adding soil to the bottom of the pot. Just add a bit of fresh cactus and succulent potting mix in the bottom of the container, loosen roots if needed, and set the rootball on the additional potting mix. The new soil level should be ½ to 1 inch below the lip of the container.

Q What kind of bird is this?

Brian Herrmann PARMA, OHIO

Kenn and Kimberly: This shy bird hiding among the branches is a fox sparrow—among the largest and most beautiful of our native sparrows in North America. They spend the winter mostly in the southern states and go far north into Canada for the summer nesting season. The key to identifying the one in your photo is the mix of gray and foxy reddish brown, which is especially bright on the tail.

Q How can I keep wasps away from the caterpillars I raise?

Margie Sloane OVIEDO, FLORIDA

Kenn and Kimberly: When we're raising caterpillars, it's sad to see them killed by parasites or eaten by predators, and it doesn't help to know that this is a normal thing. If every one of the hundreds of eggs laid by female monarchs were to hatch and survive to adulthood, we'd soon be knee-deep in butterflies. It's possible to bring caterpillars indoors and raise them in a cage or terrarium, but there's some evidence that monarchs raised indoors may have trouble navigating in their migration. You can also put a small fine mesh enclosure around outdoor milkweed plants that are hosting caterpillars to keep most insects out. That approach requires constant monitoring, however.

Q I saw a cabbage white pursuing a cloudless sulphur as it laid eggs. Was it trying to mate with it or chase it off?

James Tucker VENTURA, CALIFORNIA

Kenn and Kimberly: Some butterfly males are very territorial, perching in the open and zipping out to chase any passing flier that might be a rival male. But cabbage whites don't engage in that behavior, so this one was probably in a romantic mood. The cabbage white in your photo is a male (females sport an extra black spot on each forewing), and males spend a lot of time looking for females. Since their eyesight isn't particularly good, they make many false starts, approaching butterflies of the wrong species—or even colorful objects that aren't butterflies at all—before they find receptive females.

Q How do I discourage pigeons at my feeders?

Vivian Tester BRISTOL, TENNESSEE

Kenn and Kimberly: Pigeons can be a nuisance, especially when they arrive in large flocks, gobbling up loads of seeds. Taking your feeders down for a while is sometimes effective, but there are other options, too. Hanging feeders, especially tube style, are more difficult for pigeons to access. There also are tray-style feeders with cagelike baffles that fit over the top, designed to keep large birds from reaching the seed. Since pigeons prefer to feed on the ground, be sure to keep the area under your feeders clean as well.

Q I'd never seen a bug like this before. What kind of insect is this?

Tammy Johnson
SPRINGFIELD, MISSOURI

Kenn and Kimberly: This amazing insect—with the pattern of a bumblebee, hovering in front of flowers like a hummingbird—is actually a moth called a snowberry clearwing. It's a member of the sphinx moth family, widespread in the U.S. and Canada, mostly east of the Rockies. Unlike the majority of moths, it's active in daylight. Its caterpillars feed on the leaves of honeysuckle, dogbane and snowberry.

TAP, TAP, TAP
Like other members of the woodpecker family, northern flickers sometimes use man-made objects to drum up attention.

Q Why do woodpeckers peck at metal chimney caps? Can I prevent it?

James Gates
LEMOYNE, PENNSYLVANIA

Kenn and Kimberly: While many birds sing to claim their territories, woodpeckers have a different method. They find a dry, brittle tree limb and drum on it, hammering with rapid bursts. If they find a metal object to drum on, like your chimney cap, it may echo even more loudly than a dead branch. This is usually seasonal behavior and shouldn't last more than a few weeks. But if you want to take action, buy flexible foam or plastic padding from a hardware store and wrap it around the metal cap. The muffled sound should encourage woodpeckers to drum elsewhere.

QUAIL: GREG TUCKER; FEEDER: MICHAEL STUBBLEFIELD/ALAMY STOCK PHOTO

Q Gambel's quail keep eating my flowers. I have tried various kinds of netting, but the quail just push through and eat everything. Can you suggest a solution?
Barbie Slavkin MESA, ARIZONA

Kenn and Kimberly: Our first thought was how lucky you are to have Gambel's quail in your yard! But we can relate to the challenge of creating a habitat for wildlife and then balancing that with the need to protect garden plants and flowers. If netting has failed, you could try creating exclosures with chicken wire. Available at most farm supply stores, chicken wire is a sturdier product that might keep the quail at bay. But if exclosures fail, you may want to reconsider the plants themselves. If the quail feast on particular plants, try eliminating those flowers and planting ones less likely to appeal to hungry birds.

Q There's something growing out of the tops of my brown-eyed Susans. What could it be?

Stephen Ziring
WILLOW GROVE, PENNSYLVANIA

Melinda: This distorted growth is caused by aster yellows. This disease attacks over 300 species of plants, including rudbeckias, coneflowers, marigolds, carrots and potatoes. Aster leafhoppers carry the bacterialike organisms that cause this disease. The leafhopper feeds on an infected plant and ingests some of the organism, which it injects into the next plant it visits. This won't kill your plants, but remove any infected materials to stop the spread. Controlling leafhoppers is difficult as they're continually on the move, and spraying insecticides can harm beneficial insects that help manage pests.

Q I've fed birds for years, so why won't they visit my new thistle feeder?

David Messer LIMERICK, PENNSYLVANIA

Kenn and Kimberly: Although birds sometimes come to new feeders right away, that isn't always the case. It might just take some time for your birds to accept the new feeder. It could also be a case of stale food. Finches are very picky when it comes to thistle seed, which is also sometimes called Nyjer. They avoid seed that is not fresh. Good thistle is glossy black and clean. If the seed is old, it looks dull and dusty.

Pine siskins at thistle feeder

Q What kind of tanager is this?

Debbie McKenzie ANNISTON, ALABAMA

Kenn and Kimberly: You've captured this tanager in an intriguing stage of molt. The gray-brown streaks are the remains of juvenile plumage, just being replaced by the yellow feathers of its first-year immature plumage. Juvenile tanagers aren't even illustrated in most bird guide books, because they wear this plumage for such a brief time. At this stage, summer and scarlet tanagers can look very similar. Its bill may not be fully grown yet but it already looks too large for a scarlet tanager, and the wings don't look dark enough either. So it's a very young summer tanager, and it probably hatched not far from your yard.

Q This yellow-shafted flicker has a faint mustache. Is it a young male or female?

Rebecca Granger
BANCROFT, MICHIGAN

Kenn and Kimberly: That's a wonderful close-up photo, displaying lots of feather detail. The bird appears to be female, although it shows more contrast in the mustache area than usual. Juvenile male northern flickers (both yellow- and red-shafted forms) have a very pale orange mustache at first, which is replaced with the classic black or red mustache that adults sport before midautumn. So in late summer or early fall, we might see young male flickers with patchy mustache marks, but a bird with this subtle pattern is much more likely to be female.

SHELLING OUT GOODS

A blue jay's robust bill makes quick work of unshelled treats, like peanuts and sunflower seeds. Attract these birds to your yard by placing seeds and nuts on a tray feeder or on a flat, raised surface.

Q Sometimes I see blue jays take a peanut, scratch it into the ground and cover it with leaves. What are they doing?

Barbara Fralix
ARDMORE, TENNESSEE

Kenn and Kimberly: We often laugh about how blue jays have peanut radar. We go for days without seeing them, but minutes after we fill up the peanut feeder, the jays are back. Blue jays, along with some other members of the jay family, have a habit of caching food. When food is abundant, they take some tasty morsels and hide them away to eat later. Studies have shown they have amazing memories for finding these hidden caches, even after months have passed. So your blue jays are following their instinct to bury the peanuts for later use.

WHO'S WHO?

This is a female red-bellied—you can tell because the red mark on the back of its head doesn't extend upward toward the beak.

Q I watched a red-bellied woodpecker stick out its tongue over and over. What was it doing?

Kimberly Miskiewicz
RALEIGH, NORTH CAROLINA

Kenn and Kimberly: Red-bellied woodpeckers use their incredibly long tongues to forage for insects. They stick their tongues into tree cavities and crevices to probe for insects and grubs. The ends of their tongues are barbed to allow them to latch on to food. Sometimes they even use their tongues to drink syrupy sugar water from hummingbird feeders. Considering all the places they use their amazing tongues for feeding, they can get messy in a hurry. The bird you watched, sticking its tongue out repeatedly, was probably just cleaning its tongue after foraging.

Q Where did these holes in my tree come from?

Linette Benes NEWTON, NEW JERSEY

Kenn and Kimberly: Although we can't be certain just by looking at the photo, this may be the work of a pileated woodpecker. These big woodpeckers feast on carpenter ants, and if a tree is filled with ant colonies, the pileateds take out big sections of the trunk to get to them. Even though pileateds are large and flashy, they're surprisingly inconspicuous and out in the woods most of the time, so that could explain why you haven't seen them. It's important to realize that woodpeckers don't dig cavities in or damage healthy trees—they peck only at those already infested with ants.

Clear off the edges of heated birdbaths so visitors, like this northern cardinal, can access the water.

Q What's the best thing I can do for birds in winter?

Liza Peniston AUGUSTA, KANSAS

Kenn and Kimberly: Unless there's persistent and heavy snow cover, birds are quite adept at finding natural sources of food. But finding open water is more of a challenge. We recommend maintaining a source of clean, fresh water. In our backyard, we use a simple birdbath heater to keep water available all winter long. We've seen birds drinking and even bathing—which shouldn't cause alarm—when the temperatures are far below freezing.

Q Can I use the ashes from our winter firewood to improve my veggie garden?

Mike Murnock McKEAN, PENNSYLVANIA

Melinda: Ash does not improve drainage in garden soil. It has a high pH, so it should not be added to alkaline soils or worked in around plants like blueberries, red maples, rhododendrons and others that require acidic (low pH) soils. Have your soil tested before adding it to your garden. If the ash is from untreated wood, you can add it to the compost pile. Sprinkle some on each layer as you build your pile. The ash helps neutralize the acidic nature of compost. Don't use ash from charcoal briquettes or treated wood.

Q Should I remove the snow from drooping evergreen branches?

Juli Seyfried CINCINNATI, OHIO

Melinda: You can gently brush snow off branches after each snowfall, just avoid shaking snow off the branches. This can do more damage than the wet, heavy snow. Leave the snow in place if it's frozen to the branches. Next year, do a bit of prevention to minimize weather damage to your evergreens. Wrap multistemmed arborvitaes and junipers with bird netting or strips of cotton cloth. These hold the stems together so snow rolls off the plant instead of bending the stems.

Q Is there anything I can do in winter to improve my raised vegetable beds?

MaryAnne Katz PORTLAND, OREGON

Melinda: Incorporating compost into the soil improves drainage and adds important nutrients and organic matter that increase its water-holding ability. Compost also helps the health and vigor of plants, making them less vulnerable to insects and disease. Growing a green manure crop on raised beds is another way to improve the soil. To create a green manure, just sow buckwheat, clover, peas or winter wheat in autumn and work the plants back into the soil next spring. It's an effective way to add organic matter while crowding out cold-weather weeds. For more information on green manure, research online or call your local extension office.

MEET THE EXPERTS

Kenn and Kimberly Kaufman are the duo behind the Kaufman Field Guide series. They speak and lead bird trips all over the world.

Melinda Myers is a nationally known, award-winning garden expert, TV/radio host and author of more than 20 books.

Grow for Your Zone

Find the number associated with your region, and then stick to plants that will thrive in your area.

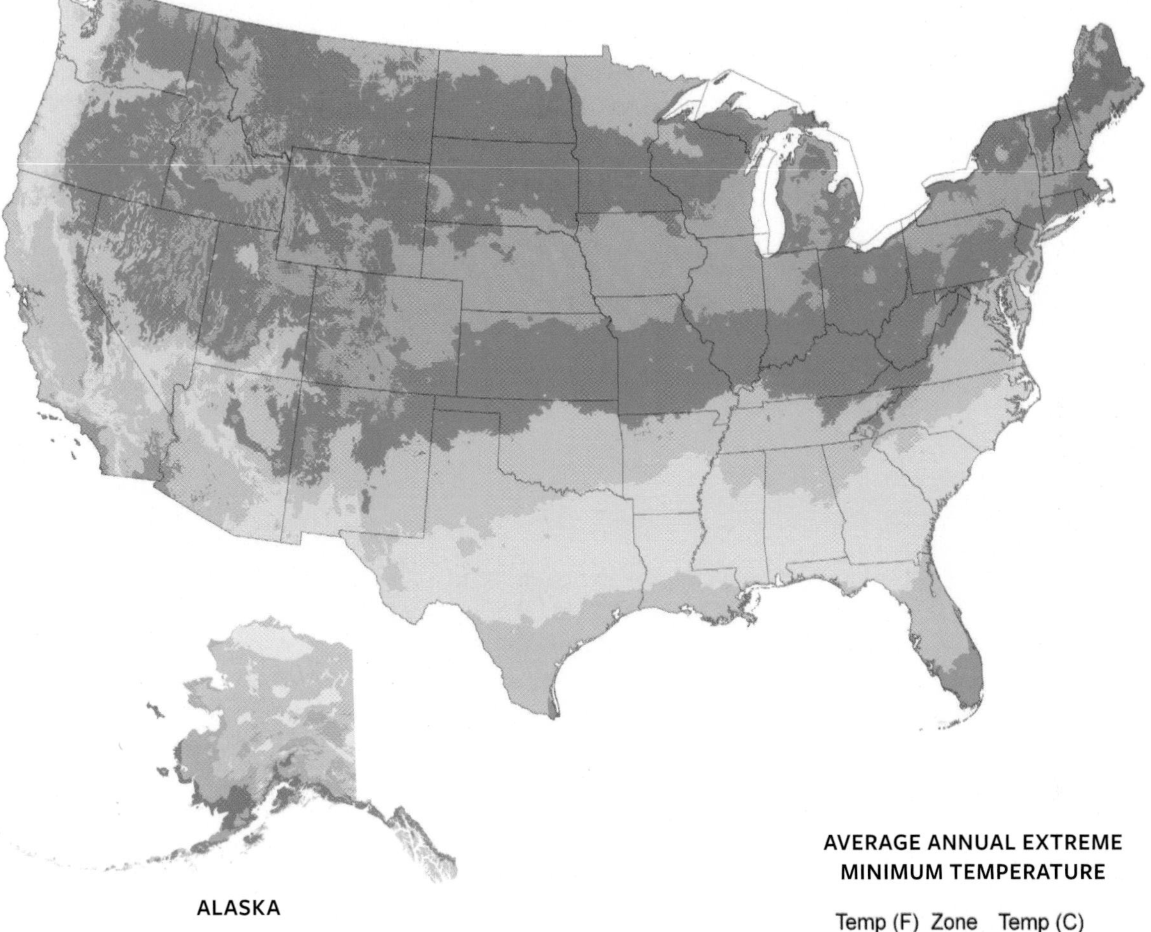

AVERAGE ANNUAL EXTREME MINIMUM TEMPERATURE

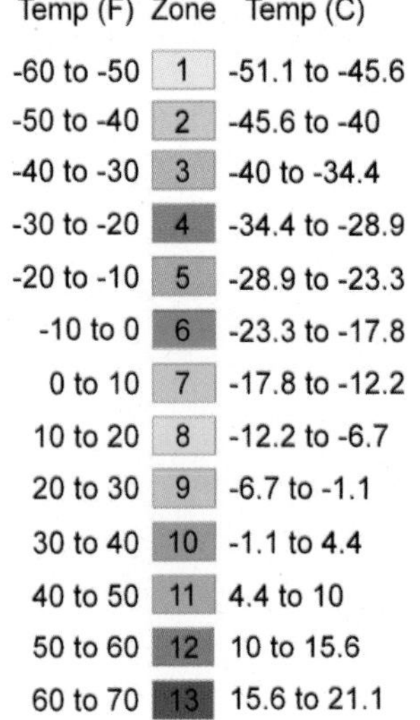

Temp (F)	Zone	Temp (C)
-60 to -50	1	-51.1 to -45.6
-50 to -40	2	-45.6 to -40
-40 to -30	3	-40 to -34.4
-30 to -20	4	-34.4 to -28.9
-20 to -10	5	-28.9 to -23.3
-10 to 0	6	-23.3 to -17.8
0 to 10	7	-17.8 to -12.2
10 to 20	8	-12.2 to -6.7
20 to 30	9	-6.7 to -1.1
30 to 40	10	-1.1 to 4.4
40 to 50	11	4.4 to 10
50 to 60	12	10 to 15.6
60 to 70	13	15.6 to 21.1

USDA PLANT HARDINESS ZONES

Hardiness zones reflect the average annual minimum cold temperatures for an area. If it's difficult to precisely locate your city on the map here, use the interactive version on the USDA's website, *planthardiness.ars.usda.gov*. After entering your ZIP code, your hardiness zone and average minimum winter temperature range will appear.

Birdhouse Guidelines

Discover which dwellings are best for your backyard birds.

SPECIES	DIMENSIONS	HOLE	PLACEMENT	COLOR	NOTES
Eastern bluebird	5x5x8″ h.	1½″ centered 6″ above floor	5-10′ high in the open; sunny area	light earth tones	likes open areas, especially facing a field
Tree swallow	5x5x6″ h.	1″ centered 4″ above floor	5-8′ high in the open; 50-100% sun	light earth tones or gray	within 2 miles of pond or lake
Purple martin	multiple apts. 6x6x6″ ea.	2⅛″ centered 2¼″ above floor	15-20′ high in the open	white	open yard without tall trees; near water
Tufted titmouse	4x4x8″ h.	1¼″	4-10′ high	light earth tones	prefers to live in or near woods
Chickadee	4x4x8″ h. or 5x5″ base	1⅛″ centered 6″ above floor	4-8′ high	light earth tones	small tree thicket
Nuthatch	4x4x10″ h.	1¼″ centered 7½″ above floor	12-25′ high on tree trunk	bark-covered or natural	prefers to live in or near woods
House wren	4x4x8″ h. or 4x6″ base	1″ centered 6″ above floor	5-10′ high on post or hung in tree	light earth tones or white	prefers lower branches of backyard trees
Northern flicker	7x7x18″ h.	2½″ centered 14″ above floor	8-20′ high	light earth tones	put 4″ of sawdust inside for nesting
Downy woodpecker	4x4x10″ h.	1¼″ centered 7½″ above floor	12-25′ high on tree trunk	simulate natural cavity	prefers own excavation; provide sawdust
Red-headed woodpecker	6x6x15″ h.	2″ centered 6-8″ above floor	8-20′ high on post or tree trunk	simulate natural cavity	needs sawdust for nesting
Wood duck	10x10x24″ h.	4x3″ elliptical 20″ above floor	2-5′ high on post over water, or 12-40′ high on tree facing water	light earth tones or natural	needs 3-4″ of sawdust or shavings for nesting
American kestrel	10x10x24″ h.	4x3″ elliptical 20″ above floor	12-40′ high on post or tree trunk	light earth tones or natural	needs open approach on edge of woodlot or in isolated tree
Screech-owl	10x10x24″ h.	4x3″ elliptical 20″ above floor	2-5′ high on post over water, or 12-40′ high on tree	light earth tones or natural	prefers open woods or edge of woodlot

Note: With the exception of wrens and purple martins, birds do not tolerate swaying birdhouses. Birdhouses should be firmly anchored to a post, a tree or the side of a building.

Source: *Garden Birds of America* by George H. Harrison. Willow Creek Press, 1996.

Nest Boxes to Know

Welcome more bird families to your backyard with a variety of cozy places for them to raise their young.

WOODPECKER HOUSE

Entice woodpeckers with boxes attached to tree trunks, from 8 to 25 feet high. Add 4 inches of wood shavings to the floor for woodpeckers to use as nesting material. The preferred entrance hole size varies by species. Downies like 1¼ inches; flickers favor 2½ inches.

SONGBIRD HOUSE

Chickadees, titmice, bluebirds and wrens are the most common backyard cavity nesters. They take up residence in classic wood birdhouses, but they're very particular about the size of the entrance hole. These songbirds are most likely to raise a family in a box if the hole is 1 to 1½ inches in diameter.

SCREECH-OWL HOUSE

Hang a box for screech-owls to nest in during summer and roost in during winter. They will use a house with an elliptical entrance hole 4 inches wide by 3 inches high. Watch them peek their heads out near dusk. Bonus! Wood ducks enjoy the same type of birdhouse.

PURPLE MARTIN HOUSE

Purple martins nest in colonies, so consider a six- to 12-cavity house. Being a martin landlord takes some commitment, though. First set up the large multiunit house 15 to 20 feet above ground—and then keep the cavities clear of nonnative house sparrows.

BUY OR BUILD

Find birdhouses at your local big-box store, or look for a pattern online and make your own.

Birds and Their Favorite Foods

	Nyjer (thistle) seed	Cracked corn	White proso millet	Black oil sunflower seed	Hulled sunflower seed	Beef suet	Fruit	Sugar water (nectar)*
Rose-breasted grosbeak				•	•			
Black-headed grosbeak				•	•			
Evening grosbeak		•	•	•	•			
Northern cardinal		•	•	•	•		•	
Indigo bunting	•				•			
Eastern towhee	•	•	•	•	•			
Dark-eyed junco	•	•	•	•	•			
White-crowned sparrow	•	•	•	•	•			
White-throated sparrow	•	•	•	•	•			
American tree sparrow	•	•	•		•			
Chipping sparrow	•	•	•		•			
Song sparrow	•	•	•		•			
House sparrow	•	•	•	•	•			
House finch	•	•	•	•	•			
Purple finch	•	•	•	•	•			
American goldfinch	•	•	•	•	•			
Pine siskin	•	•	•	•	•			
Scarlet tanager							•	•
Western tanager							•	•
Baltimore oriole							•	•
Red-winged blackbird		•		•	•			
Eastern bluebird							•	
Wood thrush							•	
American robin							•	
Gray catbird							•	
Northern mockingbird							•	
Brown thrasher							•	
Ruby-throated hummingbird								•
Anna's hummingbird								•
Broad-tailed hummingbird								•
Tufted titmouse	•			•	•	•		
Black-capped chickadee	•			•	•	•		
White-breasted nuthatch				•	•	•		
Carolina wren						•		
Cedar waxwing							•	
Woodpecker				•	•	•	•	
Scrub-jay		•		•	•	•	•	
Blue jay		•		•	•	•	•	
Mourning dove	•	•	•	•	•			
Northern bobwhite		•	•		•			
Ring-necked pheasant		•	•		•			
Canada goose		•						
Mallard		•						

* To make sugar water, mix 4 parts water with 1 part sugar. Boil, cool and serve.
Store leftovers in the refrigerator for up to a week. Change feeder nectar every three to five days.

Source: *Garden Birds of America* by George H. Harrison. Willow Creek Press, 1996.

Choose a Seed Feeder

Use an option that attracts the birds you want to spot in your backyard.

HOPPER

This classic feeder is often in the shape of a house or barn and holds enough seed to feed birds for days. Hoppers are a surefire way to offer black oil sunflower seeds to finches, jays, cardinals, buntings and other perching birds. Many have suet cages on two sides, making them all-purpose feeders for every season.

TUBE

Tube feeders are available with small ports for thistle seed or larger ports for sunflower, safflower and mixed seeds. If you want to attract small, clinging birds such as chickadees, titmice and finches, look for a tube feeder with small perches under the ports. The perches discourage bully birds and squirrels.

THISTLE

Designed to hold tiny thistle seeds (also sold as Nyjer), thistle feeders are a major draw for goldfinches. Feeders range from simple hanging mesh bags to plastic or metal tubes. You can even get ones that are a few feet long to feed an entire flock of finches or redpolls. Look for a thistle feeder that's easy to clean, as the small seeds can collect mold in enclosed tubes.

PLATFORM

These feeders hang from a tree branch or sit atop legs on the ground, and they are always completely open. This gives large birds enough space to land and eat. Sparrows, jays, juncos and blackbirds visit platform feeders, but so do squirrels.

Find feeders like these, and more, at a big-box store, garden center or specialty bird store, or online.

This Steller's jay was making the rounds of the yards in our neighborhood and demanding peanuts, which then ended up hidden in my flowerpots. What a boisterous soul!

Judy Cline SPANAWAY, WASHINGTON